D0915719

Joel R. Ridley
September 1984

ECONOMIC
FOUNDATIONS
OF
POLITICAL
POWER

The Free Press
A Division of Macmillan Publishing Co., Inc.
866 Third Avenue, New York, N.Y. 10022

Collier Macmillan Canada

Library of Congress Catalog Card Number: 73–3899

Printed in the United States of America

printing number
3 4 5 6 7 8 9 10

Library of Congress Cataloging in Publication Data

Bartlett, Randall,
    Economic foundations of political power.

    "Book evolved from a Ph.D. dissertation at Stanford University."
    Bibliography: p.
    1. Finance, Public. 2. Wealth. I. Title.
HJ135.B27   332   73-3899
ISBN 0-02-901870-6

*To my parents—
without whom
none of this
would have been
possible*

CONTENTS

PREFACE

In practice we all start our own research from the work of our predecessors, that is, we hardly ever start from scratch. But suppose we did start from scratch, what are the steps we should have to take? Obviously, in order to be able to posit to ourselves any problems at all, we should first have to visualize a distinct set of coherent phenomena as a worth-while object of our analytic efforts. In other words, analytic effort is of necessity preceded by a pre-analytic cognitive act that supplies the raw material for the analytic effort. In this book, this pre-analytic cognitive act will be called Vision. It is interesting to note that vision of this kind not only must precede historically the emergence of analytic effort in any field but also may re-enter the history of every established science each time somebody teaches us to *see* things in a light of which the source is not to be found in the facts, methods, and results of the pre-existing state of the science.

Joseph Schumpeter
History of Economic Analysis

There comes a time when brighter and brighter lights cast upon already well-lit areas yield no further illumination. Such a time seems fast approaching in the field of economic analysis. The stage upon which economists enact their dramas is a pattern of light and dark areas—ones which have been examined in depth and ones which have largely been ignored. Perhaps if we were to leave for a time the lighted areas and turn our efforts to prying open the shutters on some new windows we could begin to introduce the light that provides Schumpeter's new Vision. It would be presumptuous to set out with such a goal in mind and hence we shall make no claims of even attempting it. However, we shall make a conscious effort in the pages that follow to open a few cracks in these shutters so that we may see a vague outline of some of the forms that lie in the darkened areas. We shall leave to others the task of tearing them completely down and mapping in detail the myriad of new shapes and forms which have heretofore been delegated to the darkness between the brightly illuminated sites of analysis.

There are particular dark areas we are especially interested in exploring. One of these lies between the well-trod spaces known as microtheory and macrotheory. When Keynes published his now classic *General Theory* in 1936 it became widely recognized that government behavior was not an extension of individual behavior but was based upon different motivations and different principles. Government is a separate and powerful force in the area marked "Macrotheory." In the realm marked "Microtheory," which is but a short distance away, this recognition seems to be missing. It disappears somewhere in the dark area between. Are there any ways we can understand this mystery? What if government were an active, separate agent in the operation of the micro system as well; would we then have a better picture of the whole stage instead of just its parts? Perhaps our exploration will tell.

There is another area that interests us. Right in the middle of the brightly-lit area called "public finance" is a dark spot. The illuminated area reveals a good deal of information about how the public sector should act, and it predicts how different decisions in the public sector will affect consumers and producers, but it says almost nothing about how those decisions are reached. If we could see more of that, then we could tell which of the predicted outcomes of the lighted area is most probable.

Adventure is in our blood and we shall not even be content with examining the shape of things in the dark areas on the stage. The entire theater could be illuminated and then we could have some new perspective regarding the actual position of the economic stage. Surely we know by now that the actions of the public sector will affect the distribution of wealth and income. Not everyone gains equally. Is it possible that this is really a circle and that the distribution of wealth has some effect on the operations of the public sector? Perhaps some of the light that enters through the new cracks will give us some insight.

The script we plan to use in our search of these new areas will call for five acts. Each of these five examines one of the dark areas on the stage in some depth, but in relative isolation with regard to the others. To stop after playing out these acts would leave much still unresolved. Like a surgeon performing major surgery, we dare not quit until the patient has been successfully put back together, for only then is the job truly finished. The final chapter is thus required. Here the interrelationships among the various areas are examined and we attempt to present a broad overview of the entire drama.

Underlying the entire exploration there are three basic questions which we shall be trying to answer. We shall state them explicitly at this stage and then evaluate our success in this final act. First, we seek to understand the actual process by which tax and expenditure decisions are reached in the public sector. We ask not what should be; we seek only to discover what is. Secondly, we wish to know how this decision process affects the allocation of resources in the economy as a whole. Finally, we wish to come to an understanding of the long-run implications of the answers to the first two questions. Are there any observable relationships between the operations of the public sector and the distribution of wealth, i.e., are there relationships between economic and political power?

These are powerful questions indeed. Each is worthy of innumerable books in its own right. Hence we shall not attempt to provide even an approximation of the definitive work in these areas but shall only attempt to provide the first small bits of illumination.

Our subject matter is unorthodox at best and our method of attacking it will also be less rigorous than most current work. Admittedly the variables with which we work are not always quantifiable and the concepts we use are often too broad to assimilate easily into equation form, nevertheless we indeed agree with Paul Baran's sentiments when he states that

> . . . neither simple definitions nor refined measurements can be substituted for analytical effort and rational judgment. Yet it would certainly seem desirable to break with the time-honored tradition of academic economics of sacrificing the relevance of subject matter to the elegance of analytical method; it is better to deal imperfectly with what is important than to attain virtuoso skill in the treatment of that which does not matter.[1]

---

[1] Paul Baran, The Political Economy of Growth, Modern Reader, New York, 1957, p. 22.

ACKNOWLEDGMENTS

This book evolved from a Ph.D. dissertation at Stanford University, and as such it enjoyed the regular attention of my reading committee. Professors John Gurley, Robert Coen, and Michael Boskin made significant contributions to the work. Moreover, their support of my choice of an unusual topic allowed me a measure of satisfaction in my work that would have been lacking in a more conventional inquiry. Many of the ideas in this book are the result of the comments and suggestions they have made, and hence they should share the credit, and probably even some of the blame, for its content.

Similarly, a number of my fellow graduate students at Stanford endured all or portions of the manuscript at various stages in its development, and a number of their comments have been incorporated into this final draft. Included in this category are Steven Brenner, William Powar, Edward Ray, and Phillip Perry. Mrs. Lillian Zabahon provided much welcomed assistance in satisfying all the administrative details required by the University.

It is a hard economic fact of life that even in the pursuit of knowledge one requires food and shelter. I am indebted to the Committee on Arms Control and Disarmament Dissertation Research of the National Research Council for their generous assistance in obtaining these essentials. It is my sincere hope that they realize an acceptable return on their investment.

Finally, in spite of the texture of library stacks and academic seminars which tend to surround it, a book is written in a larger context of living. In this broader area many people have contributed unknowingly to the completion of this work. I owe a most special word of thanks to C.P., who provided me with an unending supply of encouragement when I had to work, and an undeserved, but greatly appreciated, amount of happiness when I didn't.

ECONOMIC FOUNDATIONS OF POLITICAL POWER

INTRODUCTION

> Positive economics is in principle independent of any particular ethical
> position or normative judgments. As Keynes says, it deals with "what is,"
> not with "what ought to be." Its task is to provide a system of generali-
> zations that can be used to make correct predictions about the conse-
> quences of any change in circumstances.
>
> **Milton Friedman**

Few economic topics generate greater passion and more political controversy than questions about what governments should purchase
and who should be made to pay for these purchases. Taxes, the major
form of payment, are the primary mechanism for adjusting the income
distribution of a society; and certainly in the United States cries for tax
reform are a traditional ingredient of political campaigns. Heated de-
bates over the "ordering of national priorities" are in effect simply de-
bates over the patterns of governmental purchasing, i.e., over the directions in which we channel our resources. Certainly the presidential
election in 1972 demonstrated a concern with these issues; center stage
of Senator McGovern's platform was given to a call for a redistribution
of tax burdens and a reordering of spending priorities. Certainly the
tremendous political controversy arising from President Nixon's budget
proposals for fiscal 1974 demonstrates the intensity with which different groups in society view these issues. And surely we dare not forget
that at the bottom of each such controversy are human beings whose
ability to deal with the material demands of modern society is greatly
affected by the outcome.

The science of economics turns its potent tools of analysis to
these very questions with some regularity in an attempt to determine,
in somewhat abstract terms, guidelines for reaching prescriptive answers
based on criteria of "equity" and "efficiency." Yet these guidelines do
not measure up to the standards of positive science outlined by Pro-
fessor Friedman, for they deal largely with determining what policy
"ought to be" and indeed offer almost no help in predicting what the
outcome of the policy decision process will be. We need to distinguish
most clearly between those theories which design a perfect world and
those which instead help describe our own quite imperfect one. The
distinction is, of course, the one between normative and positive analysis; it is the distinction between determining what the ideal tax structure would look like and determining the forces that keep the actual

structure from being ideal. In understanding reality, significant attention must be paid to questions like the latter, but so far such inquiries seem to lie outside the traditional boundaries of "economic analysis." Part I of this book attempts to modify the tenets of prescriptive normative analysis in order to make them more amenable to description. Parts II through V apply the modified tenets in the hope of forming the basis of a new positive theory of governmental actions in a market economy.

CHAPTER 1
THE DEVELOPMENT
OF A
POSITIVE SYSTEM

Then let us begin and create in idea a State; and yet the true creator is necessity, who is the mother of invention.

Plato

We will be concerned, in the pages that follow, with the operations of a market system which contains a significant public sector. The questions that we have raised center on how such a system operates as opposed to how it should operate. Since this is a topic that has been largely ignored for a long time in economic analysis, much of the work will be original in nature, but, like most original work, it has roots deeply imbedded in that which has come before. Therefore, in establishing the structure of our positive system it will be beneficial to consider explicitly these roots, and to point out the way in which the new structure differs from the older ones. These roots, we shall see, are almost exclusively normative in nature yet too often they carry the implicit connotation that that which should be also is. In our new system, we shall reverse this characteristic and attempt to discuss that which is, explicitly avoiding the question as to its desirability in ethical terms.

Let us begin by stating in very simple terms the theoretical operations of a market system and the justification for utilizing a collective body to improve these operations. We shall then trace certain modifications made by others, and add a few essential modifications of our own. The end result, it is hoped, will be a model, an approximation of reality, which allows us to explain and understand the phenomena which surround us in our economic and political world.

THE STANDARD APPROACH IN SIMPLE FORM

As any student of elementary economics knows, a market system of economic organization is based upon the decentralized decisions of rational consumers and producers, each operating in his own self-interest.

Consumers desire to attain the highest possible level of total utility by consuming goods and services which possess subjectively desirable qualities. They are limited in their ability to maximize utility by the existence of a binding budget constraint. Few individuals have the means to satisfy all their conceivable wants. Therefore, in order to attain the highest level of utility possible under this constraint, they will offer money for goods and services in amounts which represent the relative intensity of their desire for particular items. In more formal terms, utility maximization leads consumers to acquire goods in proportions such that the marginal rate of substitution between any pair of goods is equal to the ratio of their prices. If this condition is not satisfied, there is a potential increase in utility attainable.

Producers, on the other hand, are assumed to be profit maximizers who utilize real resources to create goods and services which can be sold at a profit to consumers. If they are to achieve their postulated goal, they must use these limited resources in the production of goods for which consumers are willing to pay the highest prices. This automatically causes resources to flow into those uses where they make the greatest possible contribution to the maximization of consumers' utility. No centralized decisions are necessary for the entire system to work smoothly in a well coordinated fashion.

Proponents of this view of market operations have existed and argued in defense of it for hundreds of years. Adam Smith's famed invisible hand which drove selfish individuals to promote the public good while in pursuit of their own ends is a timeless illustration of the principle. Yet not even the most abstracted of contemporary analysts would claim that this presents a sufficiently accurate picture of all operations. Economic systems, like everything else on a human plane, suffer from certain imperfections which inhibit the free movement of this invisible hand.

To the extent that we find imperfect competition, significant externalities, increasing returns to scale, and goods that exhibit a greater or lesser degree of "publicness," we can no longer expect to achieve a position of optimality, defined in Paretian[1] terms, through the unhin-

---

[1] Pareto Optimality, deriving its name from Italian economist Vilfredo Pareto, is a term applied to a social situation in which no individual can improve his welfare without reducing another individual's. Whenever one person can gain without harming anyone else, it is an unequivocal improvement in social welfare for him to do so under Paretian criteria.

dered operations of the market. Such an optimum is normally reached when it is no longer possible to improve the position of one actor in the economic drama without injuring another. In formal terms this means that starting with given production functions and fixed utility functions, a position of social optimality will be reached when the marginal rates of substitution in both production and consumption are equated to the price ratios for all pairs of goods. The presence of one or more of the above difficulties effectively blocks the path to such an optimum and requires non-market action for correction.

Musgrave outlines a number of situations where the presence of these obstacles requires some form of collective action.[2] For example, if markets exist which exhibit imperfect competition, then there will be restrictions on the flow of resources into those markets when changes in demand occur. As a result excess profits will be maintained over the long run, prices will not all be set at marginal cost and a non-optimal position will be maintained. In order to reach Pareto optimality some form of collective action, either legal or market, will be required.

Another case where the market suffers from failure is when there are significant externalities present in the production of some commodity. For example, if the smoke from a factory is causing damage to the residences or the health of neighboring individuals to the extent that they could realize a net gain by paying to have the smoke reduced or eliminated, the attainment of Pareto optimality requires that they do so. However, it is not likely that any one individual can afford the costs of smoke elimination by himself, but a distribution of the costs among all the beneficiaries may reduce the costs per individual to an acceptable level. Such a distribution requires a collective group with a certain degree of coercion over its members, however, if it is to be effective. Otherwise, each individual would attempt to escape his share of the burden while still enjoying the benefits of smoke elimination.

A third example of market failure occurs when the production process of some industry exhibits increasing returns to scale over a range of operations to the extent that marginal cost pricing would result in heavy losses to the producer. Once again, the market solution to such a situation is sub-optimal, and the presence of a non-market agent

[2] Richard Musgrave, *The Theory of Public Finance*, McGraw-Hill, New York, 1959, pp. 6–8.

administering a program of tax and subsidy would allow an improvement over the market solution.[3]

A distinguishing factor in all of these cases, however, is that the difficulties in terms of efficient market operation can all be ameliorated without any concrete *market* action on the part of the collective body or government. It can enforce the free entry of firms into an industry through legal action; it need not actually enter the industry itself. Similarly in the other cases it can utilize programs of transfer payments as solutions; it need not actually utilize resources to produce commodities nor does it need to actually consume goods and services.

Nearly all economists would concede the necessity for some form of government to establish the "rules of the game" and to correct for market failures.

> The role of government just considered is to do something that the market cannot do for itself, namely, to determine, arbitrate, and enforce the rules of the game. We may also want to do through government some things that might conceivably be done through the market but that technical or similar conditions render it difficult to do in that way. . . . There are two general classes of such cases: monopoly and similar market imperfections, and neighborhood effects.[4]

There exists another form of market imperfection which cannot be remedied by indirect action, but which requires instead direct participation of the government in the operations of the economic system. This imperfection arises whenever there are goods present which, because of a quality of "non-excludibility," exhibit a significant degree of "publicness." Samuelson has defined a public good as one

> . . . which all enjoy in common in the sense that each individual's consumption of such a good leads to no subtraction from any other individual's consumption of that good so that [equal amounts are consumed] simultaneously for each and every i^{th} individual and each collective consumption good.[5]

Others have been less restrictive in their definition of what constitutes a public good. Otto Eckstein has claimed that public goods:

[3] Cf. Wm. S. Vickrey, *Microstatics,* Harcourt, Brace and World, New York, 1964, pp. 249–259; also Musgrave, *op. cit.,* pp. 136–140.

[4] Milton Friedman, *Capitalism and Freedom,* McGraw-Hill, New York, 1962, pp. 27–28.

[5] Paul A. Samuelson, "The Pure Theory of Public Expenditures," *Review of Economics and Statistics,* November 1954, p. 387.

Some analysts include still one more category of goods which must be provided in the public sector if an optimal situation is to be attained. This consists of those goods which Musgrave would title "merit wants," i.e., wants ". . . considered so meritorious that their satisfaction is provided for through the public budget, over and above what is provided for through the market and paid for by private buyers."[11]

The inclusion of goods of this type obviously involves a rather severe value judgment since it requires interference with consumer preferences. Therefore, since we wish to avoid value judgments in this work, we shall ignore the presence of goods which are included in the public sphere because they have been found to be ethically desirable by some sector of the population. Government in our model will arise because of the market imperfections outlined above, and because of the presence of purely or partially public goods.

We have now laid out the elements of the simple standard model of government action in a market system. The nature of this system can be seen in the accompanying diagram. It initially consists of two groups, producers and consumers, pushing from opposite sides of the market. The former are pursuing profits and the latter utility. In a perfect world the system would settle on a point of maximum welfare such as *W*, as the inevitable result of purely self-interested, decentralized decisions.

Yet imperfections and public goods exist, and their presence introduces "leakages" into the flow of the system towards an optimal solution. Government is then used as a sort of "plug," a "deus ex machina," to eliminate the difficulties that this presence creates. It is assumed, as we have seen, that government is merely a frictionless process allowing consumers to pursue utility collectively rather than

[11] Musgrave, *op. cit.*, p. 13.

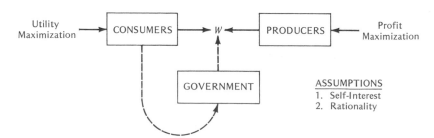

individually. Its introduction is regarded as an effective means of countering the leakages and it thus acts as a force which will help to return the system to an optimal point such as W.

The optimism which such a picture of the world generates has been countered in part by the work of a few analysts who have felt modifications were necessary in the operations of the system as depicted in the diagram. Let us turn briefly to a discussion of their work, and then move on to the additional modifications we shall introduce in our development of a positive model.

Logic and chronology do not always travel in the same ordered paths, however. Analysts of the problems of public action ordered according to one system of succession will not necessarily form the same line that would result from the other. On occasion, aspects of these problems which follow in close logical sequence have been examined according to a time schedule of moving quickly ahead, returning later to fill the gaps left behind. We examine the modifications made in the standard system following the sequence suggested by logic, keeping in mind the qualification that some of the work done on "later" aspects of the problem was completed earlier in time.

EARLY ALTERATIONS IN THE STANDARD APPROACH

An observer of the standard system would come to an early recognition of the fact that some method of aggregating consumer preferences is necessary in the public realm. Even if government is merely a name for the collective action of consumers, and if government decisions are "the collective decisions of individuals," we still need some process of reaching these decisions. If we are unable efficiently to aggregate the desires of the individuals making up the state, then this inefficiency will be reflected in the allocation of resources which is affected by collective action.

It was in a discussion of this very problem that Arrow's pioneering work in the area of social choice poked the first pin through the bubble of optimism inflated by the standard approach.[12] The proof of his "possibility theorem" introduced a serious amount of friction into the governmental machine view that Buchanan and Tullock postulated above. In this work, Arrow establishes what he considers to be the

[12] Kenneth Arrow, *Social Choice and Individual Values* (Second Edition), John Wiley and Sons, New York, 1963.

minimum conditions of a situation of "collective rationality" and then he concludes that with at least three possible choices, there can be no method of aggregating preferences under majority rule that simultaneously satisfies these conditions and the principle of voter sovereignty.

In its simplest form the Arrow problem centers around the fact that with three or more options to be voted on, and with at least one voter preferring extremes to moderate positions, the outcome selected will depend on the order in which the alternative pairs are considered. No one choice can be viewed as "best" from the point of view of aggregate society since there always exists a possible order of voting which can defeat any particular option. The outcome in such a situation is always arbitrary and, according to Arrow's criteria, it is therefore not a choice made by a process of rational decision making. In his words, the conclusion to be drawn from proving his theorem is as follows:

> If we exclude the possibility of interpersonal comparisons of utility, then the only methods of passing from individual tastes to social preference which will be satisfactory and which will be defined for a wide range of sets of individual orderings are either imposed or dictatorial.[13]

The introduction of this difficulty presents a serious obstacle to the effective operation of the system. If simple majority voting is used to determine collective choices, then these will reflect either an absence of voter sovereignty or a violation of Arrow's conditions of rationality.

This problem is almost universally acknowledged by authors working in the area of public finance, but it is generally regarded as a technical difficulty to be overcome, rather than as a serious defect. Richard Musgrave looks at the problem in this manner.

> A technique must be found by which individuals are induced to reveal their preferences for social wants (even though the exclusion principle cannot be applied) and by which a choice can be made among all the solutions that are optimal in the Pareto sense. Without this, neither the benefit nor the ability-to-pay approach has much content.[14]

To Musgrave this is essentially a two-part problem.

> We are concerned not only with finding a consistent solution on the basis of given data but with finding a technique by which individuals can be induced to reveal their true preferences on matters of budget policy. . . . The trick, then, is to find the type of voting process that gives us the best approximation to a result based on true evaluations.[15]

[13] *Ibid.,* p. 59.
[14] Musgrave, *op. cit.,* p. 116.
[15] *Ibid.,* p. 117.

Musgrave then examines the efficiency of a number of different voting procedures in different situations, e.g., simple majority voting with a single service budget and fixed tax shares in order to determine the budget size. In all of these hypothetical situations he assumes that voters do not engage in strategic behavior in an attempt to increase their own benefit from the collective decision. Within the confines of this assumption, he concludes that point voting[16] is the process best able to approximate an optimal solution.

> We may expect such a system to give determinate results over a wider range of cases than the plurality rule and to give better reflection of underlying preferences. This holds for a comparison with plurality rule and even more so with majority rule.[17]

Strategy cannot be ignored, however, because the central reason for utilizing public rather than private choice is that voters cannot be expected to reveal their true preferences for collective goods. This is because the benefits from public goods must be distributed independently of the nature of individuals' contributions to their acquisition. As a result "majority voting may be the better system, even though point voting would be superior in the absence of strategy."[18] This conclusion on the part of Musgrave is really an admission of partial failure in his search for an accurate means of aggregating preference. He stated earlier that such a failure would imply that "neither the benefit nor the ability-to-pay approach has much content."

Others have made the process of reaching collective decisions a more central part of their analyses. Buchanan and Tullock introduce the need of finding an efficient means of aggregating preferences within the confines of decision-making costs as well as under the problem of non-reavealed preferences.[19] Musgrave and Arrow centered their discussions around a technical problem of mechanically aggregating preferences without explicitly considering the costs involved in this aggrega-

---

[16] "Point" voting is a system that allows an individual to express the intensity of his feeling for different alternatives. Each individual is given a fixed number of points before the voting process begins, and he can allocate them among the different proposals, presumably giving a large number of points to the options he desires most. In the extreme case where he intensely desires one outcome over all others, he may allocate all of his voting "points" to a single alternative.

[17] *Ibid.*, p. 131.

[18] *Ibid.*, p. 132.

[19] James Buchanan and Gordon Tullock, *The Calculus of Consent*, University of Michigan Press, Ann Arbor, 1962; paperback 1965.

tion process. If our system, even in its simplest form, is to be consistent, then the rational, self-interested consumers at its core will attempt to minimize these costs as well as to influence the outcome of the decision in their favor. According to Buchanan and Tullock it is this desire for cost minimization that leads first to less than unanimous decision rules, and then to an abdication of the right to directly participate in most collective decisions.

In their scheme, the costs of reaching a decision increase with the number of individuals involved in making it. Dictatorial government is not acceptable however, because there is, in opposition to these costs, a range of possible "external costs" which an individual may have to bear as a result of collective decisions over which he has no influence. These expected external costs are assumed to fall as the number of individuals necessary for decisions rises. They become equal to zero when complete unanimity is required. Individuals agree to less than unanimous decision making, however, because they are trying to minimize the combination of decision making and external costs. Under such a situation the possibilities of reaching Pareto optimality are extremely limited, and the possibility of being able to choose among optimal points (as Arrow wished to do) are almost nil.

The introduction of decision-making costs creates a further obstacle to the attainment of an optimal position, even if the purpose and desire of government is to do nothing else. This obstacle arises from the fact that it would be grossly inefficient for most consumers to participate in collective purchasing decisions at all. It would be utterly absurd for 200 million people to engage in a process of aggregating preferences with regard to the purchase of a typewriter to be used in providing some public good. The share of the purchase price borne by each consumer would be far less than his share of the costs of reaching such a decision. As a result, the rational, self-interested consumers will abdicate the throne of absolute consumer sovereignty, and delegate the authority to make their collective purchasing decisions to representatives.

> Direct democracy, under almost any decision-making rule, becomes too costly in other than very small political units when more than a few isolated issues must be considered. The costs of decision-making become too large relative to the possible reductions in expected external costs that collective action might produce.[20]

[20] *Ibid.*, p. 213.

The use of representatives reduces the decision-making cost function by reducing the number of individuals who must reach agreement before a collective decision is made. The actual consumers of collective action will still play a part in collective choice according to Buchanan and Tullock, by influencing the choice of representatives. At the same time, they will have attempted to protect their interests when the system of government was first established. Once representation has been decided upon, the group must establish rules for choosing representatives, and they must establish the method by which these representatives will reach decisions. Moreover, the degree of representation must be chosen, as must the rules for determining the basis for representation.[21] The careful manipulation of these variables at the time of constitutional choice provides consumers with a measure of control over the direction of collective choice, while the ability to influence representatives through voting lets them affect these choices even after abdication of their authority.

At this stage in the development of our positive model, the shining image of government as the panacea for the imperfections of the market has become slightly tarnished. Consumers do not directly participate in most collective decisions, and even if they did, we have no means of aggregating their preferences such that we can find an acceptable guide to collective actions. Even maintaining the assumption that government's sole purpose is to provide individuals with a means of attaining their individual objectives through collective action we would have to conclude that it suffers from gross inefficiency in realizing this end. To be sure, it may be better than a market with no form of collective body, but it is far from perfection.

Before going any further in the development of our model, we should perhaps examine the logical consistency of the standard approach as it has been modified so far. All individuals are rational in this system, and all are motivated by their own self-interest. Certain members of the system are chosen as representatives of other rational, self-interested individuals and are endowed with the power to make collective decisions. These representatives function in the market in a capacity which differs from that of either traditional consumers or producers. Their primary role lies within the government, and their primary identification and classification must reflect this. These individuals actively seek office, and

21 *Ibid.*, pp. 213–214.

we can observe them going to great effort and expense in order to attain it. This fact points to a serious inconsistency within the system as it has been developed so far. We must conclude on the basis of this set of facts that either government individuals do not seek their own self-interest but are motivated by a desire to maximize consumers' utility, or they too adhere to the principle of self-interest which implies that they act in a manner designed to reach their own goal, which *is* the attainment of office. In the first case, the assumption of self-interest which is at the very heart of a market system would have to be abandoned. In the second, the view of government as a functional extension of consumers has to be abandoned. The system must somehow be modified to eliminate the inconsistency that this situation presents.

Downs recognized this dilemma and chose the second way out as the better of the two. He considered government and the political parties from which a government is chosen to be a distinct group in the market, separated from the consumer sector, rather than as a portion of it.[22] This obviously required the introduction of a new motivating force since the maximization of consumer utility was no longer acceptable. Downs claimed that government would establish policies with an eye towards getting elected, rather than seeking election in order to establish some ideal state of the world. Government, and political parties became vote maximizers in his theory, just as producers are profit maximizers.

He turned, from this initial alteration, to an examination of the optimal strategies for vote maximizing political parties, and to the effects of uncertainty on the behavior of parties and voters. His primary concern, however, was over the voter-party interaction, and producers entered the political arena mostly in the capacity of a special type of voter. The introduction of this completely new force was an extremely important step in the development of a positive model of the public sector, but it was too often ignored in the later literature.

---

[22] Anthony Downs, *An Economic Theory of Democracy,* Harper and Row, New York, 1957. This book by Downs is one of the few works that uses economic tools to examine governmental actions from a positive as opposed to normative view. His book is often noted, but the implications of his analysis are too often bypassed—the work and its implications deserve more attention by economists.

THE POSITIVE MODEL

The positive model with which we shall be working has its roots in much of this earlier work, but from these beginnings it has developed significant differences in form. There are three major alterations from the specification of the standard model as it was outlined in the diagram on page 10. We shall look at these alterations in turn. But first it is necessary to say a few words about models in general. Economists often use the term "trade-off" to describe a choice between two inversely related variables. If you decide to have more of one thing, it implies less of the other. The use of models as tools for positive description carries with it a trade-off between reality and manageability. A decision which too heavily favors one or the other of these will render the analysis nearly useless.

In the real world, wherever that may be, an infinite number of variables operate in an infinite number of relationships to determine the whole of what we call "reality." Some of these relationships are of marginal significance to the outcome, and so in an effort to reduce the analysis of reality to manageable proportions we concentrate on only the most important variables. This makes the problem simple enough to handle, but makes it into a model which is a less than perfect picture of reality. The major difficulty in this approach to understanding is that the selection of variables must be an *ex ante* decision, i.e., we must decide what to study before undertaking the analysis. We cannot analyze the whole of reality and then decide what is and what is not important.

As a result the use of models entails a risk. It is possible that in the creation of a theoretical system we may be eliminating some variables which are not marginal, but are absolutely crucial to the problem at hand. One of the complaints we have with the earlier work is that it was limited to a rather narrow definition of the problem and hence excluded a consideration of several variables which are of central importance to the understanding of "reality." In our decision to use a model, we have placed ourselves in a precarious position, for there is no guarantee that we have chosen the appropriate variables for study. It is quite possible that the specification we have chosen is, in itself, guilty of the short-comings of which we have accused our predecessors. For example, in our decisions to limit analysis of agents to a single role, e.g., producer, consumer, etc., we are effectively excluding the dual nature of individual's roles; this duality, particularly in the public sector, may be of far more than marginal significance.

Aware of the problems involved, we have nevertheless chosen to adopt a model in our study at the cost of making the analysis a less than perfect picture of reality. Our model is closer to reality than the standard one, and our conclusions should also approximate reality more closely. The trade-off between reality and manageability is unavoidable and we have made our choice within the boundaries of this constraint. We are aware of the problems this presents; the reader should also be aware of them.

The standard model we presented consisted of two major assumptions concerning the behavior of individuals, self-interest and rationality, and the specification of two opposing groups, consumers and producers. In addition there was a subset of consumers, a government, which was a collective process aimed at facilitating consumer utility maximization. Our model differs from this in several respects.

Economic Men in Government

In our model we shall adopt Downs' specified motivation for government, the attainment of office. In a democratic government this implies that decisions be made with an eye toward the expected effects of different alternatives on the voting behavior of the electorate. For Downs this meant that governments and political parties are vote-maximizers, and we shall follow his lead in adopting this assumption.

There are of course other possible assumptions that carry the same idea of vote consciousness on the part of the collective body. For example, government could attempt to maximize its vote share or percentage of votes which is not always the same as maximizing votes. It could act in such a manner that it appeared to be maintaining a simple majority rather than maximizing votes absolutely or it could have a number of other similar motivations.[23] All of these motivations center around one particular characteristic, the fact that government is operating in its own self-interest as are the other agents in the system. It is

---

[23] For a brief listing of possible alternatives see Bruno Frey and Lawrence Lau, "Towards a Mathematical Model of Government Behavior." Reprint No. 59 from Research Center for Economic Growth, Stanford University. Pp. 357–358.

this idea which makes the difference in the system important; the choice between similar versions of expressing the difference is of marginal importance at best. Any one of the other assumed motivations would yield nearly identical conclusions. Hence we have maintained Downs' assumption since it is at least as good as any of the others, and perhaps better.[24]

Since we claim to be developing a positive model, we should perhaps take time to consider the normative implications of accepting the justification for government's existence that was used in the standard model. In that model government was introduced in an effort to overcome the difficulties presented by market imperfections. From the very beginning it was assumed to be universally desirable.

Not every observer of, or participant in, the political process has subscribed to this view of government's purpose and function. James Madison, who had a certain amount of practical experience in the operation and creation of government, wrote,

> The diversity in the faculties of men, from which the rights of property originate, is not less an insuperable obstacle to a uniformity of interests. *The protection of these faculties is the first object of government.* From the protection of different and unequal faculties of acquiring property, the possession of different degrees and kinds of property immediately results; and from the influence of these on the sentiments and views of the respective proprietors, ensues a division of society into different interests and parties. . . . The most common and durable source of factions has been the various and unequal distribution of property. Those who hold and those who are without property have ever formed distinct interests in society. . . . The regulation of these various and interfering interests forms the principal task of modern legislation, and involves the

---

[24] There are three reasons why vote maximization may be the best option available to approximate reality. (1) Governments are highly uncertain as to their actual vote position prior to the date of election. It can be altered by opposition party tactics up until the last minute. Hence vote maximization will allow a margin of safety to protect against last minute shifts in voter behavior. (2) The margin of victory for the winning party is directly related to the degree of power it enjoys, at least during the early days of its term in office. The more votes a party has, the more powerful it is. (3) V. O. Key has shown that voter behavior over time, and even intergenerationally is largely a matter of habit. The more voters a party can get to identify themselves as members of the party, the more secure is the long-run position of that party. It has a larger block of votes which it can count on. The larger the vote in any one election, then, the better the chances in succeeding elections.

"bureaucracy" which is driven by a desire to maximize its own "bureaucratic security."

One manifestation of this desire will be reflected in the view bureaucrats will take toward their budgeting decisions. The size and rate of growth of a bureau's budget are the most easily arrived at measures of a bureau's worth. Since a bureau deemed of great importance will provide security for its members, their actions will often reflect an attempt to increase both the size and rate of growth of their particular bureau's budget.

This seems a cynical view of public servants at best. Surely, it may be argued, there are some who really feel that the work they perform and the services they provide are meaningful contributions to social welfare, and it is this conviction which motivates them. But, if this belief leads them to work vigorously to increase the size and power of their particular agency so that they may more effectively perform this valuable service, then the effect in terms of behavior is exactly the same as that produced by self-interested security maximizers. The important point is that bureaucrats are most concerned with the bureaus they comprise; consumers are most concerned with the utility they enjoy. There is no mechanism which automatically brings the two concerns together. There are, of course, limits to how far bureaucratic actions may diverge from consumers desires, and we shall explore them as we proceed. This is not the same as saying that the two will be coincidental however.

At any rate, our positive model has expanded the groups which participate in the market from two to four. Each has a specific motivation which determines its behavior. Each interacts with, and hence is constrained in, its operations by the other three groups. Occasionally, this interaction will inhibit the attainment of a groups' goals; on other occasions it will facilitate it.

The Basic Assumptions Reconsidered

The standard model contained two behavioral assumptions at its very core: the assumption of rationality on the part of all agents, and an assumption of self-interest as the central characteristic of agents' motivations. We shall retain both of these assumptions in our positive model, but we shall add to them a third assumption whose implications will prove to be most significant.

Before introducing this third assumption, let us take a few minutes to clarify what we mean by "rational" and "self-interest." The assumption of rationality is necessary if we are to derive any meaningful conclusions about the behavior of individuals. Without some form of consistency in the pattern of human behavior it would be futile to attempt to understand and predict social phenomena. It is important to emphasize, however, that our definition of rationality carries no normative connotation regarding the ethical desirability of any particular set of goals. By rational we mean only that the course of action taken by any agent will be an attempt to move closer to, rather than farther from, the attainment of whatever goal that agent has chosen. In other words, we assume that an agent who is faced with a given set of options and with a set of expectations as to the effects of choosing each option, will choose that one which he thinks will bring him closest to his goal. A particular agent may be bent on self destruction and yet this can be consistent with our assumption of rationality if that agent's actions always reflect choices which he feels increase the likelihood of his attaining that goal.

Due to uncertainty and a lack of pertinent information, an agent may occasionally make an incorrect choice in terms of reaching his goal, but as long as he *expected* his choice to be beneficial, he acted rationally. A rational individual bent upon suicide will not purchase and consume an antidote to poison he has taken. An individual who is *not* suicidal but still consumes poison is still rational if he thought that the product was a utility producing good. Unfortunately, this individual's ability to judge accurately the actual utility of the product will not develop until after the fact; it may not develop until after his death. Rationality in the actions of economic agents refers to the strategy used to attain their ends; it does not apply to the ends themselves.

Self-interest is also assumed to underlie human behavior. By this we do not mean to imply that there is never any altruism in human society; there is ample evidence of its presence. We shall define self-interest sufficiently broadly for individuals to derive utility from charitable endeavors, but we shall assume that these are marginal operations. Individuals may make small contributions to the well-being of others, but we assume that this will occur only when the costs of so doing are relatively small. For example, an individual agent may contribute to the Community Chest, but he will not, in our system, willingly give his entire income to producers with no goods presented in exchange. Indeed, if agents do not operate in their own self-interest, however they may define it, the entire concept of a market system becomes meaningless. It cannot be expected to allocate resources in anything but a random manner. Self-interest, broadly defined will be a central motivation in our system. No agent can be as concerned with the problems of all other individuals in the world as he is with his own; no agent will be able to ignore completely his own welfare.

To these two assumptions it is now time to add a third. Models of perfect competition assume a degree of knowledge on the part of all agents that approaches perfection. If there is any one thing we can agree upon from an observation of real phenomena it is that all individuals are certain to be uncertain! A positive model which attempts to explain that which is must begin by creating a picture of the world in which decisions are made in an atmosphere of imperfect information. We shall thus postulate as our third central assumption that all agents in the positive system will suffer from a greater or lesser degree of uncertainty relative to the economic and political decisions they must make. Theorists have often admitted the necessity of including uncertainty, but have seldom included it in sufficient degree.

> . . . the amount of information that is, in principle, required for the strict application of the theorem (of perfect information) is substantially greater and more varied, detailed and exact, than we are likely to find in practice.[30]

Admissions such as these are generally nothing more than parenthetical insertions in long discourses on systems with assumed perfected knowledge.

The alterations in the operation of a system when imperfect information is introduced are so great as to render models based on perfect information largely irrelevant. A model to be useful must be more than internally consistent; it must bear some direct relation to reality since that is what models are purported to be explaining.

Uncertainty is so prevalent in the real world for two reasons. First, the total universe of knowledge, even in the most practical sense of the word, is so utterly immense that no human agent has the mental capacity to assimilate even a small part of it. Each individual has the ability to be in possession of only a relatively few facts at any point in

---

[30] William Vickrey, *Microstatics*, Harcourt, Brace and World, New York, 1964, p. 219.

time. He will limit himself to the acquisition of those facts which he regards as most relevant to the decisions with which he is faced, e.g., it is more important for an Illinois farmer to be aware of present and predicted wheat prices in the Chicago market than it is for him to know the proverbial price of eggs in Russia.

However, even if he were to limit himself to directly relevant facts, the total body of information would still exceed his capacity to assimilate it. The farmer in our example could not possibly know the actual amount of rain to be expected in different parts of the country over the next growing season, the amount of wheat each farmer will plant, the amount that will grow, the likelihood of disease, the nature of consumer demand in the future, etc. He, like all agents in a realistic system, will have to make his decisions on the basis of less than perfect information, i.e., under the constraint of uncertainty.

Uncertainty is made greater, secondly, by the costs of acquiring information. An agent attempting to reduce uncertainty will actively seek information, but this process involves real and direct costs. These may take the form of the expenses involved in direct scientific research, the purchase and analysis of library materials, etc., or they may result only from time inputs. In this second case, we witness a fairly large amount of information offered through the mass media which requires no direct investment on the part of the individual acquiring it, save for the time input involved in assimilating it. As economists we must still regard this as a real cost in the opportunity sense, however, so that the acquisition of any information entails expenses.

The result of this fact is that the amount of information it is rational for an agent to acquire is even less than the amount he is capable of absorbing. He will operate under the ever present constraint of uncertainty, and we must explicitly include this in our model. To ignore it would be like explaining the motion of the human body without considering the role of the skeleton as well as of the muscles. It would be intellectually interesting, no doubt, but puzzlingly ineffective in application.

THE MODEL RESTATED

We have now made three significant changes in the model that was outlined in the diagram on page 10.

1. Government has become a completely new classification. It is no

longer merely an extension of consumers but operates like all other groups of agents, in its own self-interest. This implies that it will follow a vote maximization strategy in determining policies.

2. There is a fourth classification of agents known as the "bureaucracy" which also is driven by its self-interest. In this case, this implies that it is attempting to maximize bureaucratic security.

3. In addition to an assumption of rationality and one of self-interest on the part of all participants in the model, we have also assumed that all agents must labor under the constraint of uncertainty.

The new system, which is the basis for our positive analysis, can be depicted as follows:

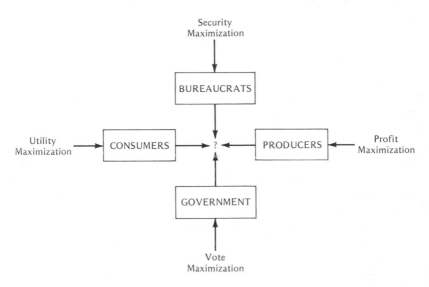

The question we have to examine is what effects the specification of the system in this manner will have on the ability of the system to attain an optimal point W. In addition, this new specification calls into question the definition of what constitutes an optimal point. Both of these questions require rather extensive analysis, and we devote the remainder of the book to the search for answers.

CHAPTER 2
UNCERTAINTY
AND INFLUENCE

No man is an island, entire of itself. . . .
John Donne

The addition of the third basic assumption needs to be considered further, for it carries with it an unavoidable complication—the pervading potential for the production of influence. An agent who is constrained by the assumption of uncertainty and who is faced with the necessity of making a decision needs to consider the possible costs involved in making an incorrect decision, i.e., one which he would not make with perfect information. On the other hand, he also needs to consider the real costs involved in acquiring information with which to reduce or eliminate this uncertainty. There are costs in being informed and costs in not being informed. The rational agent will have to strike some balance between the two types of cost. This balance will lead to a limited amount of information that it is rational to acquire before reaching a decision, and the decision will be based upon this imperfect stock of information. To the extent that an interested external agent is able to affect the acquisition of information, he will be able to influence the decision and hence the behavior of the agent in question. Most often this influence will result from the ability of the influencer to change the relative prices of different types of information faced by the decision maker. The process of influence production is not only economic in nature, it also will alter the behavior of all agents in the economic and political system of our new model from that which occurred in the standard model. For this reason, let us examine the process in some detail.

The Process in Some Detail

The subject of decision making under uncertainty is not unknown to economists. The approach usually taken to the problem, however, is to assume that decisions are made on the basis of certain probability distributions as seen by the decision maker. He then attempts to maximize his expected utility within the future world which these distributions

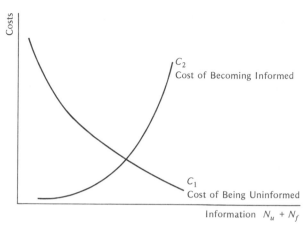

Figure 1

reach a choice between X and Y[2]. Define "p" as the probability that X is the correct choice and that "$1 - p$" is the probability that Y is the correct choice, both probabilities estimated by B. Then we can say that

$$p = p\left(\frac{N_u}{N_f}\right), \tag{1}$$

[2] Subjective probability depends not on the actual chance any outcome has but on the chance you think it has. As any horse-player can tell you, the two will often differ.

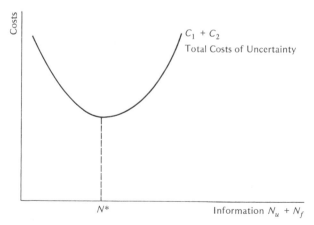

Figure 2

where N_u is information which is unfavorable to decision Y and N_f is information favorable to Y. If we assume that the cost functions for the two types of information are identical, B will acquire equal quantities (but not necessarily equally weighted) of both, N_{u_o} and N_{f_o}. Let us say that

$$p\left(\frac{N_{u_o}}{N_{f_o}}\right) > 1/2$$

so that B chooses alternative X, the choice he would have made under certainty. In this case, the assumption of uncertainty has added little more than inconvenience to the problem, but let us change the situation slightly and introduce influence.

Influence Production.   Return now to the point in time when B was first faced with the decision, but before he had engaged in the acquisition of any information. There now arrives on the scene a second agent who will play an important role in the process of choice. In order to accommodate this second individual, it will be necessary to add a few new assumptions to the four previously postulated.

5.   There is a second individual, A, who is affected by B's decision.
6.   A will be better off if Y is chosen than if X is chosen. A may be a producer interested in a consumption decision, a politician interested in a voting decision, or even a thief interested in the decision of a jury. The possibilities are unlimited.
7.   A possesses a certain amount of information relevant to B's decision, and he is able to separate it into two parts: N_f, which is favorable to decision Y, and N_u, which is unfavorable to it.
8.   A has no means of coercing B into reaching decision Y, but A may subsidize B in his acquisition of information.
9.   B makes no ex ante distinction between the quality of subsidized information relative to non-subsidized information.

Under these additional assumptions B will again be faced with the necessity of balancing the two types of costs against one another in his search for the optimal position. This still occurs where his total costs are minimized, or where the marginal cost of an additional bit of information is equal to the expected marginal gain from acquiring it. However, A may now take action aimed at altering both the total stock of information it is rational for B to acquire and also the composition of that stock at this optimal point.

We can best see these alterations by analyzing the "purchase" of information in a form that is analogous to the normal approach to the behavior of a discriminating monopolist.[3] In Figures 3a and 3b we have shown the marginal and average costs of acquiring N_f and N_u respectively. Initially, assume that the costs are approximately equal, i.e.,

[3] We are indebted to Prof. R. Coen for first suggesting this type of approach to the problem of analyzing influence production.

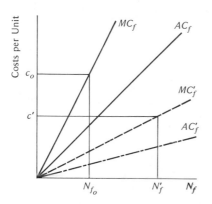

Figure 3a

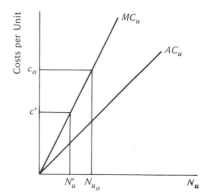

Figure 3b

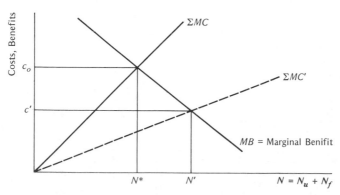

Figure 3c

the MC_f and AC_f curves are relevant. We can horizontally sum the marginal cost curves for the two "markets" and derive the ΣMC curve of Figure 3c. The optimum point in terms of cost minimization is then found at the intersection of MB and ΣMC. Information should be acquired until the marginal gain from an additional bit just equals c_0. This implies a total stock of information N^* which is equal to $N_{f_0} + N_{u_0}$.

If A wished to provide B with an incentive to acquire relatively more N_f, he could lower the costs to B of acquiring such information. Then the appropriate curves for analysis in Figure 3a become MC_f' and AC_f' and the ΣMC curve in Figure 3c becomes $\Sigma MC'$, the horizontal sum of MC_f' and MC_u'. The optimum position is now found by examining the intersection of this curve with the marginal benefit curve. The amount of information it is rational to acquire is now found where the addition to benefits just equals c', i.e., where the stock of information equals $N' > N^*$. Moreover, the composition of this optimum stock will now be different. $N' = N_f' + N_u'$ where we can see that $N_f' > N_{f_0}$ and $N_u' < N_{u_0}$. In other words, B will react to the subsidization of N_f by acquiring more of it, both relatively and absolutely, than he would in the absence of such behavior on the part of agent A.

Hence, not only has the size of the optimal stock of information changed, but still more important, the composition of that stock has also changed in response to A's activity. The significance of this fact becomes apparent when we realize that it now implies that

$$p\left(\frac{N_{u_0}}{N_{f_0}}\right) > p\left(\frac{N_u'}{N_f'}\right) \quad \text{since} \quad \frac{dp}{dN_u} > 0 \quad \text{and} \quad \frac{dp}{dN_f} < 0.$$

If the ratio of N_u to N_f has been reduced sufficiently, the value of p will now fall below $\frac{1}{2}$ and the value of $(1 - p)$ will exceed $\frac{1}{2}$. B will now choose alternative Y, even though this would be the "wrong" decision if he had costless access to all information. His response to a change in the relative price of selected information has lead him to an incorrect decision.

This is essentially the "Blind Date Problem." If my cousin is coming to town and I want my friend to take her out, I subsidize his acquisition of the information that she had a charming personality and beautiful blue eyes. I neglect to tell him that she has three of them and weighs some four hundred pounds. My subsidization of selective information is aimed at leading him to a conclusion he quite possibly would not reach if he had all the relevant facts at his disposal.[4] However, his experiences with me as a source of information in this one case may lead him to distrust somewhat my accounts of things when I present them at other times in the future. On the basis of my past performance he may tend to discount the information that I provide him at reduced cost. We can easily include such a discount factor in the analysis that we have been developing.

Discounting Subsidized Information.   For the sake of realism, then, let us drop assumption (9) and replace it with a more plausible postulate:

9'.   B applies a constant discount factor d to all information whose acquisition is directly subsidized. The magnitude of d will depend upon a variety of factors including B's past experience, his personality, and his awareness of A's interest in the decision, but it will always be less than one.

This discount factor will reduce the *effective* stock of N_f influencing B's decision below the level of the actual stock, and will thus raise the cost of altering B's decision. The variable which becomes important now is the effective amount of N_f which B will acquire. We define this by:

$$N_f^e = dN_f \quad \text{where} \quad d < 1 \tag{2}$$

Now B's decision depends on the ratio of this variable to N_u, i.e.,

$$p = p\left(\frac{N_u}{N_f^e}\right) = p\left(\frac{N_u}{dN_f}\right) \tag{1''}$$

The alteration of probability estimates necessary to change B's decision now requires a greater amount of subsidized information. Figure 4 illustrates the relationship between p and N_f for a given amount of N_u, and N_f' indicates the amount of subsidized information necessary to make $p < \frac{1}{2}$. The introduction of a discount factor shifts the function to the line FG and now the amount of subsidized information required rises to N_f''. This implies a higher cost to A, since presumably the provision of more information will lead to an increase in the total costs of subsidization. If influence production is to be feasible there will thus have to be a higher minimum gain to A from choice Y

---

[4] Mark D. Herrero and Alice I. W. Sweeny of Stanford University should be noted for providing me with empirical evidence of this phenomenon.

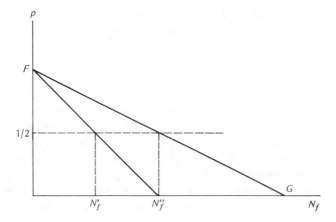

Figure 4

than there was previously. If d becomes small enough, the amount of subsidization necessary for effective influence may lead to prohibitive costs, but as long as $d > 0$ influence through information pricing is at least possible.

Moreover, whenever A's *ex ante* estimation of the gain from influence is greater than the costs of producing it, our assumption of rationality requires him to engage in influence production. In any economic and political system the number of decisions made by one agent that affect the welfare of another is extremely great. Therefore, we would expect to see this process of influence at work in many decisions in such a system. All the agents in our model operate under uncertainty, and as a result of this they are all susceptible to influence through information pricing in many of their decisions.

SUMMARY OF THE POSITIVE MODEL

Economic theory has attempted to introduce a public sector into its analyses by making certain marginal changes in its previous models. For the most part, these models were of a normative nature, and this bias is generally reflected in the modifications. Economic models of government describe how it should operate in order to foster economic efficiency; yet this has often been at the expense of being able to describe accurately how government does work. There are many phenomena in the real world of politico-economic systems which cannot be explained within the framework of this normative theory.

It is our avowed purpose to overcome this shortcoming at least in part. We have made a concession to manageability by adopting a model of our own in order to examine these phenomena, but we have attempted to make this model positive rather than normative in nature. We chose our groups of agents on the basis of simple observation— we can see that they exist. We make no *ex ante* judgments on whether or not their existence is desirable from an economic point of view. Our concern is what happens to the economic system when these agents and groups of agents interact.

We have restructured the usual economic model to include four groups of agents, each group basing its actions upon a different goal. These groups are:

1. consumers, who are attempting to maximize their own utility;
2. government, which is attempting to maximize the votes it receives;
3. producers, who are attempting to maximize profits; and
4. bureaucrats, who are attempting to maximize their own security.

Moreover, there are three basic assumptions underlying the behavior of each of these groups:

1. All agents are primarily motivated by their own self-interest.
2. All agents are rational in the pursuit of this self-interest.
3. All agents labor under the constraint of uncertainty, and hence all agents are subject to influence in the making of market and political choices through the medium of information subsidization.

In a world built along these lines any number of conclusions made on the basis of conventional theory must be re-examined. The alterations we have made will have far-reaching implications for all areas of economic theory. We have not set for ourselves the task of writing the definitive work examining all of these implications—we will be concerned with only a few of them. We turn our attention to four distinct problems and leave the countless other problems to other authors.

We begin by examining the nature and effects of public purchasing decisions made within this environment, and then, secondly, we consider the means by which these purchases will be financed. The third area of concern centers around the problem of non-voting influence—its production and its producers. Finally, we attempt to examine the wider picture of society concentrating on the effects and results of unequal distributions of wealth, and the relationships between these and the system we have been developing.

We have set for ourselves a formidable task and one which is not without pitfalls. We have developed a vehicle with which to pursue it and we have established an itinerary. The journey before us is long; and the preparations have, at times, been tedious. Let us thus begin.

PART
II
POSITIVE
PRINCIPLES
OF
PUBLIC
PURCHASING

INTRODUCTION

The economic history of the United States in the twentieth century has been very much a story of a growing public sector. Over the course of the last forty years the purchase of real goods and services by governmental units grew from approximately 8% of Gross National Product to nearly one-fourth (22+%) of total output by 1971. State and local government expenditures rose from 7% to 13% of GNP while expenditures by the federal government exhibited a much larger rate of growth, rising from 1% to 9% of GNP in the same period. It is apparent that governmental units are assuming a position of increasing significance in the determination of final demand patterns in the United States, and the picture in the other large countries of the world is quite similar.

It is a simple fact that governments purchase real goods and services and that these purchases affect the welfare of members of society. We have seen that governments come into being in democratically organized societies in part because of the high costs of reaching collective decisions in large groups. These decision-making costs are reduced by the utilization of representatives who make collective decisions and allocate costs and benefits among the members of the electorate. Since elected representatives in our positive model can not make this allocation decision directly on the basis of simply aggregated consumer preferences, it is obvious that the process of governmental decision making will be of great importance in determining the welfare of individuals.

It is important to keep in mind that it is the total *net* effect of government action on the welfare of members of the society which is the crucial variable. The estimation of this net effect requires the simultaneous examination of both taxes and benefits from public expenditures with regard to each individual and cannot be determined by examining expenditures or taxation in isolation. A particular pattern of public purchases may imply either a net decline or a net increase in the welfare of particular individuals depending on the nature of the tax program which finances it. Buchanan stresses the equity ramifications of this fact:

> If a major share of governmental expenditures were allocated to provide protection to the property rights of the wealthy classes, then even a progressive tax system might not prevent the fiscal system from increasing real income inequality.[1]

[1] James Buchanan, *Fiscal Theory and Political Economy*, University of North Carolina Press, Chapel Hill, 1960, p. 20.

Nevertheless, we witness a separation of the decision to purchase particular items from the decision to implement particular forms of tax financing. As a result we shall analyze the two decisions in isolation. In the synthesis at the conclusion of the book, we shall reconsider this question of net effects but for the time being we assume the tax structure to be given. The problem is to determine what goods will be purchased with the revenues gathered from the taxpayers within the context of this structure.

Each of the four groups of our positive model will have an interest in the solution to this problem, and each of them will participate in the decision-making process in one manner or another. We turn now to an examination of the behavior of these groups and to an analysis of their participation in the determination of public purchases, starting with consumers and moving counterclockwise around the diagram of the positive model on page 26.

CHAPTER 3
CONSUMER
BEHAVIOR

> The survival of democracy depends on the ability of large numbers of people to make realistic choices in the light of adequate information.
>
> **Aldous Huxley**
>
> ... for a great many citizens in a democracy, rational behavior excludes any investment whatever in political information per se.
>
> **Anthony Downs**

In our model society there exists a large body of individuals who play active roles in both the public and private sectors. When functioning in the latter area we call them consumers; when functioning in the former we call them voters. In order to simplify matters we shall assume the two terms to be synonymous, implying that the memberships of the two categories are coincident. To be sure producers, bureaucrats, and government officials all vote, but this is not their primary means of influencing public decisions. Nothing more is lost in the use of this assumption than is lost by ignoring the fact that producers also consume goods and services.

These "consumer-voters" must be regarded as direct participants in the operation of the private market and in the choice of governments and public policies. In the former, they spend money for real utility-producing goods and services and, in the latter, they "spend" votes for an expected stream of benefits to be derived from the collective actions of government. In both realms the primary motivation of consumers is the maximization of utility, but unlike the consumers of earlier models, the utility functions upon which they base their actions can no longer be regarded as fixed over time and devoid of external influence in their formation. In our positive analysis we have to consider explicitly the economic phenomenon of producing changes in utility functions.

CONSUMERS IN THE MARKET

> We only know that when a consumer faces a given set of prices and income, he will always choose the same set of commodity bundles which satisfies his budget constraint.[1]

[1] Shin-Yen Wu and J. Pontney, *An Introduction to Modern Demand Theory*, Random House, New York, 1967, pp. 112–113.

It seems to have become customary, if not compulsory, in economic analysis to begin studies of consumer behavior with the assumption that preferences are given and constant over time.[2] Whatever the method by which consumers form their particular preference functions, it is usually regarded as a process which is not appropriate for study within the context of an economic system. It is our contention that first of all preferences are not static but change over time, and secondly, that they are indeed subject to outside influence in this change. Moreover, this process of influencing preferences and through them the economic behavior of various agents is an inescapable aspect of the rational pursuit of economic and political goals.

Continued reliance on this assumption amounts to academic isolationism, for its adoption excludes some of the major conclusions of developmental and social psychology, sociology, and cultural anthropology. These are all concerned with an individual's values, perceptions, and desires and the way in which he forms them. Studies in these fields all lead to similar conclusions—that all individuals exist in a cultural and sociological environment and owe much of their perception of the world and many of their reactions to its phenomena to this environment and other individuals who share it.

There are both large scale and small scale values which are influenced by this environment. The largest ones are reflected in personality characteristics which tend to be dominant among particular national groups; the smallest ones are reflected in faddish demands for minor items.

The culture into which an individual organism is born will determine, to a large extent, the personality which it will develop. This is so basic to anthropology as to be almost definitional:

> Children, when they are born, are without culture, and hence are without personality, and almost without social relationships. The very fact of birth may be described as the termination of a biophysical relationship and, in the usual course of events, its replacement with a social relationship. Social relationships, then, expand with maturation; new culture is demanded in which to respond to other people so that the relationships are possible. The acquisition of that culture is ipso facto the growth of personality.[3]

[2] Occasionally, economists admit that this assumption is inaccurate. Cf., for example, Tibor Scitovsky, "On the Principle of Consumer Sovereignty," *A.E.A. Papers and Proceedings*, May 1962, pp. 262–268.

[3] Paul Bohannan, *Social Anthropology*, Holt, Rinehart and Winston, New York, 1963, p. 20.

This personality, coupled with the basic value system that the culture inculcates, will affect the value in utility terms that different goods have for different individuals. The utility which an American citizen might derive from an American flag is a direct result of cultural training. The same organism transplanted at birth to a rural Asian peasant culture would derive far different utility from the same physical object.

Political scientists are sometimes aware of this:

> Any well-knit way of life molds human behavior in its own design. The individualism of bourgeois society like the communism of a socialized state must be inculcated from the nursery to the grave. . . .[4]

Even an occasional economist stresses the fact that preference functions arise out of the cultural environment:

> The truth is that wants of people are complex historical phenomena reflecting the dialectic interaction of their physiological requirements on the one hand, and the prevailing social and economic order on the other.[5]

Obviously, such extensive influences need not be considered in the short run problem of choice between commodities. In these limited studies variables such as culture and personality may be taken as given without seriously affecting the results. It is only when we are concerned with the long run structure of society and the relationships between classes within the society that the influencing of preferences on this scale becomes important. We shall delay our analysis of this larger problem until Part V.

Even in the short run, however, there is a good deal of evidence that the preferences for different marketable commodities are learned and subject to external influence. In some cases this influence may be effective for very short periods only before being countered by experience, but in other cases it may be more or less permanent. In all cases, it arises because of the presence of the uncertainty which pervades our entire model, and it often takes the form of information subsidization.

There is an additional dimension of the purchasing decision that is seldom included in analysis—time. Market behavior takes place over time and the relative positions of different variables within the

---

[4] Harold Laswell, *Politics: Who Gets What, When, How,* Meridian Books, Cleveland, 1958, p. 32.

[5] Paul Baran, *Political Economy of Growth,* Modern Reader, New York, 1957, p. xvi.

time spectrum change the behavior of agents even though the magnitude of the variables may be the same in a variety of different time positions. In terms of purchasing decisions, the act of purchasing does not coincide with the act of consumption in most cases, and particularly in the case of durable goods. Because of this the decision to buy is made on the basis of the expected utility of consumption and not on the basis of actual utility. The two values need not coincide in the presence of uncertainty. Anyone who has ever purchased a used car is aware of the potential difference between what you think you are getting and what you actually get.

The expected value of consuming good i in period $t + 1$ as seen at the time of purchase, t, is the crucial variable. This expected value will be a function of the actual utility of consumption of similar commodities in the past and also of information acquired as a result of nonconsumption activities. In the case of an article purchased with some regularity over the past, the expected and actual values of utility will approach equality as the previously purchased items provide a constant feedback as to the validity of the original expected value.

For example, the purchase and consumption of milk in the past will provide a housewife with strong empirical evidence as to the utility of consuming different quantities of this product. On the basis of this evidence she can have confidence in her ex ante purchasing decisions for milk, and we, as observers of her economic choices, can be confident that they accurately reflect her actual utility function.

However, if the item in question is not one which is regularly purchased, or is one which is in some way qualitatively different from similar commodities purchased in the past, then there arises the strong possibility of a divergence between expected and actual utility at the time of the purchase decision. In this case the market behavior which we observe is indicative of expected utility only. To the extent that producers, or anyone else with an interest in consumer choice, can introduce such a divergence, they may be able to alter consumers' behavior in their favor. In fact, the rationality assumption of our model implies that they will attempt to influence consumer choice and that consumers will be affected by this influence whenever the gains to the influencer exceed his costs.

Consumers' susceptibility to influence arises because uncertainty is definitely an undesirable situation from their point of view since it introduces the possibility of incurring real costs by making an incorrect purchasing decision. It is to their advantage to reduce the chances of incurring these costs by eliminating uncertainty prior to the act of purchase. As with all situations where information is not without costs of its own, there is only a limited amount it is rational to acquire. This is essentially an example of the general situation outlined in Part I, Chapter 2. This implies that the presence of uncertainty will result in the purchase of many goods being made on the basis of imperfect information, i.e., without full awareness of the actual utility that these goods will yield in consumption.

Producers and their selling agents may then see an opportunity to improve their own positions by consciously altering consumers' stock of information in a selective manner in an effort to influence purchasing decisions. This can be done most easily by subsidizing the acquisition of information favorable to the producers' ends. The consumers, attempting to minimize costs, will accept this information though they may apply a greater or lesser discount factor to it. This is essentially the nature of advertising, and we can see that most of it is provided to consumers at a subsidized rate. We need not search as far for an example of this type of behavior as an itinerant peddler of patent medicines, but since it is an interesting one we shall use it anyway. By informing his audience of the wonders of his miracle potion in curing all known diseases of man, he may be able to alter their estimation of the utility to be derived from his product and hence increase their purchases of it. They will not realize their actual utility of consumption until after the purchase has been made and the product tested. In the event that it turns out to have been seriously overrated, the peddler's utility function probably specifies that he should be long gone at the time of this discovery.

Kevin Lancaster, in an article analyzing consumption as an analogue to production, demonstrated an awareness of this process:

> In consumption, as in production, the prime reasons for inefficient use of the existing technology are ignorance and lack of managerial skill. The consumer may not be aware that a certain good possesses certain characteristics or that certain goods may be used in a particular combination to give a specified bundle of characteristics. Producers or sellers may use advertising to ensure that no characteristics of their product regarded as particularly desirable should go unnoticed by consumers. They will go to less pains to ensure that consumers are aware of some other characteristics of their product.[6]

[6] Kevin Lancaster, "Change and Innovation in the Technology of Consumption," *American Economic Review*, May 1966, pp. 14–23, p. 18.

Of course, consumers will be able to make better estimates of utility *ex post*, and this revised estimate may affect future purchasing decisions of the same or similar products. In this case the process may be self-correcting and the induced divergence will disappear over time; the introduced distortion may be regarded as a situation of disequilibrium.

However, if there are social characteristics of the good, then even if the consumer is able to accurately estimate his private utility from the item in question, *ex post*, he still may not be able to estimate the total utility. For example, we could look at gasolines. A consumer will be able to determine the mileage he gets from different brands, and perhaps the changes in performance, but he will not really be able to accurately estimate the contribution of particular gasoline brands to reduced air pollution. Even though he may consume the product, he must still rely on externally provided information in his attempts at evaluating the utility he derives from the social characteristics of the good.

Moreover, if the good is seldom purchased, there may be no opportunity for correction of estimates and the distortion will be essentially permanent. This will be the case with durable goods which are subject to product differentiation, e.g., color TV's, hi-fi's, perhaps even homes. The influencing of consumer preferences has resulted in the long run diminuation of consumers' potential utility incomes but a gain for the influencer.

Changes in Actual Utility. There are also a number of examples of permanent changes in actual utility of consumption that derive directly from this process of influence production. For the most part, these depend upon the subsidization of two distinct types of information by interested nonconsuming agents. This subsidized information may either create a need for a particular product, or affix characteristics to a good which are not really inherent to it. In either case utility functions, once changed, will not necessarily be altered by experience with the product. If the influence has been successful then the actual utility of consumption will be altered as well as the expected utility.

The first type of subsidized information, i.e., that which creates a need, may be used for any number of products. Beyond the simplest requirements for food, shelter, and clothing, man's needs are really indeterminate in any absolute sense. The use of information may allow external agents to affect these needs. For example, during the hottest part of the "cold war" there was a large demand for bomb shelters by individual consumers. The utility that they derived from these was in large part a result of information they acquired as to the possibility of enemy attack and their increased chances of survival in such an event given a shelter. Both of these probabilities may have been somewhat influenced by outside agents, including contractors who build shelters. It seems somewhat implausible that the need for such an item arose simultaneously, yet independently, in so many individuals. Indeed, the purchase by one man may have reinforced his neighbor's decision to buy which in turn verified his own, but from the point of view of any one man, much of the utility of bomb shelters was learned.

This same process of need creation may be found with regard to items of far less serious consequence, for example, certain types of gum. Recent advertising campaigns have warned against the dangers of "ho-hum mouth" and "nothing breath." It is no longer sufficient to avoid bad breath; now there is a need to create a freshness of breath by using particular products. The utility derived from these products has to be regarded as at least partially learned.

The second type of subsidized information is also widespread. We can see evidence of it in the case of double breasted suits. A few years ago these items of clothing held very little utility for most American consumers, but now that the quality "being in fashion" has been affixed to them, that utility has risen substantially. Once again, it seems likely that this was, in part, a learned response rather than an independent one when examined from the point of view of a single consumer. Perhaps "being in fashion" has always been a part of the utility function, one might argue, and hence we can escape the dilemma by claiming that the function hasn't really changed at all. But the escape is illusory. Whether the function changes, or its relationships to market goods changes, is immaterial. What is important from the economic point of view is the choice of particular market goods and if this choice changes over time, it doesn't really matter whether the change was caused by an alteration of the utility function or an altered relationship between it and goods. In either case, the effects on market behavior are the same.

An examination of advertising will provide a great deal of evidence of this type of information subsidization. Very little advertising stresses the actual physical characteristics of goods; most stresses non-inherent qualities. Toothpastes provide sex appeal, automobiles provide status, and mouth washes provide job promotions—truly astonishing technical advances in the field of chemistry, or rather obvious examples of influence being exerted on utility functions.

Costs of Influence. To be sure, there are real costs involved in producing influence which must be borne by the influencer, but there are also real gains to be made in many cases. As long as the influencer's *ex ante* estimation of the benefits is greater than his estimation of the costs, then our postulate of rationality requires him to attempt to produce influence. The presence of a discount factor applied to the subsidized information involved will obviously raise the costs of influencing to the influencer, and the more extreme the discount, the greater the rise in costs. These costs require that a potential influencer have the resources with which to subsidize information as well as the desire to do so.

Under these conditions we would expect to see producers engaged in substantial amounts of influence aimed at altering consumers' utility functions and hence the demand curves they face; we would not expect to see consumers engaged in the acquisition of nonsubsidized information to counter this influence. This is so because only a small part of any consumer's income goes toward the purchase of a particular good while all of a producer's profits come from the sale of that good. A producer has more to gain from increasing sales than a single consumer has to lose, particularly when there are significant economies of scale in the dissemination of subsidized information.

Take, for example, the case of a producer who purchases television time to provide consumers with selective information about his product in an attempt to alter their expected and perhaps even actual utility. Once the contract is signed there is a total cost to the producer of some amount, K, which is not then affected by marginal changes in the audience. If on the basis of the information disseminated, each consumer who watches the show reappraises his expected utility of consumption (this may be toward either a more or a less accurate estimation) such that his observed *MRS* with other goods is altered and he buys an extra unit of the good at price p, the producers costs of influence may be justified. This will be the case if enough consumers are so influenced that the sum of their extra expenditures exceeds the sum of K and the extra costs of production. Since the producer receives income from each of the consumers, economies of scale have made it rational for him to purchase the television time.

For consumers, however, the cost of making a wrong purchase in most consuming decisions is not great enough to justify the acquisition of much nonsubsidized information. The amount of income going into each particular purchase is relatively small. Hence producers will often present selective information which is not countered by consumers acquisitions of unbiased, unsubsidized information. Consumer choice will often be affected as a result.

This assymmetry between producers and consumers in the influence of purchasing decisions is also the result of certain characteristics of consumption information. Much of the information pertaining to consumer choices which could counter the influence of producers displays several of the peculiar qualities of public goods.[7] For example, once I incur the costs of carefully researching the quality of different items it becomes difficult to provide this information to select consumers only. Once I sell my findings to some consumers they take on the quality of publicness which accompanies non-excludible goods. I can no longer limit the consumption of this information to those who help meet the costs of originally acquiring it. It thus becomes irrational to subscribe to such information if there is the possibility that other agents will meet the costs while I also enjoy the benefits. The lack of excludibility that accompanies much consumer information makes collective action aimed at providing it unlikely on a voluntary basis.[8]

Summary. Consumers' utility functions still determine their actions within the confines of the private market, but these utility functions are at least partially endogenous. Consumers learn of "needs" for new goods and also of "qualities" of goods from information subsidized by producers. Whenever producers have a sufficient monetary incentive to engage in influence as measured by the difference between benefits and costs, and whenever they have sufficient resources to finance the production of influence, our postulate of rationality requires that they do so. This same postulate implies that consumers will not counter this

---

[7] Thanks once again are due to Prof. Robert Coen for first pointing out this phenomenon.

[8] We include a more careful discussion of the rationality of collective action in large groups of small agents in Part IV of this work when we discuss the work Mancur Olson has done in this particular area.

influence with non-subsidized information, and hence their market choices are at least partially the result of the actions of external agents.

CONSUMERS IN THE PUBLIC SECTOR

Consumers not only purchase goods in the private market; as we have seen, they also acquire a certain number of goods collectively. The need to do this may arise from the presence of public goods or because of market imperfections, but for whatever reason, we can witness the action of collective bodies in the market. At the same time that we introduced the need for collective action, we introduced the necessity of administering collective action by indirect means. The costs of reaching decisions in large groups of individuals will generally exceed any gain that could be expected from direct participation in the process. Hence it is rational for consumers to use representatives to make their decisions in the public sector thus reducing the costs of reaching these decisions.

The decisions made by these representatives are generally binding, however, and hence there is still an incentive for attempting to influence them in order to avoid externally imposed costs. Consumers maintain the power to remove representatives whose actions appear to be too costly by using periodic elections to express general approval or disapproval. In these elections they spend "votes" in an effort to extract the greatest possible utility from collective actions much as they spend money to acquire utility producing goods in the private market. We maintain the assumption of utility maximization in this aspect of consumer behavior as well. However, as in the case of the private market, there are peculiar aspects of this utility which warrant rather extensive examination.

Downs on the Voting Decision.   Anthony Downs went to some effort to analyze the nature of a voter's decision. It will help our analysis first to outline his conclusions and then to re-examine them in the light of our positive model. For Downs the voting decision in a democracy is based upon a "party differential."[9] He defines a utility income from government action over the interelection period and claims that voters' perceptions of this utility will be the determining factor in voting. There

[9] Cf. Downs, *op. cit.*, esp. Chapter 3.

a result of this increase in subsidized information provided by the Democratic party.[11]

Isolation and Influence in the Public Sector. The consumption of most public goods involves a degree of "isolation" which is not found in the private market. Many goods consumed collectively have a minimal direct and observable impact on the average consumer. For example, few individuals come into direct contact with an Anti-Ballistic Missile system. Its existence is known to them but they have no way of directly evaluating its effectiveness and worth. Similarly, most taxpayers do not have any real contact with a system of publicly financed higher education. They are dependent upon external sources for an evaluation of the worth and effectiveness of such a system.

This isolation is present to a greater or a lesser degree in nearly all publicly purchased commodities and it carries with it the potential for even more influence of utility functions than we witnessed in the private market. This influence affects both the expected and the perceived actual utility of public goods. Agents who have an interest in public purchasing decisions or consumers' evaluations of these decisions may create influence by subsidizing information as to the need for particular products and programs, the expected effectiveness of particular products to fulfill these needs, or the *ex post* effectiveness of previously purchased products.

For example, producers or bureaucrats who have an interest in the establishment of an ABM system may create first a need for it in the public mind by providing information as to the first strike capability and intent of the Soviets and, secondly, information as to the ability of particular systems to thwart this intent. From the point of view of the individual consumer who must contribute for the purchase of such a system, its utility is almost totally dependent upon external information. He has no way of knowing the intent of the Russians nor does he have the technical capability to evaluate the data on Russian missiles and the data on the proposed ABM. He learns that a need exists and that there is a product which will fulfill it.

Similarly, he is susceptible to influence in the formulation of *ex post* estimates of actual utility. Once created, the utility he derives

---

[11] For an account of this aspect of the election, cf. Bruce Page, G. Hodgson, and Lewis Chester, *An American Melodrama*, The Viking Press, New York, 1969, esp. pp. 711–735.

from the ABM depends upon how much safer he *feels* from enemy attack rather than how much safer he is. He has no way of evaluating this latter variable in the absence of a real attempted attack. The utility he holds depends on externally provided information since he lacks access to technical data and the ability to evaluate it if he had it. A government which has approved such a product must then attempt to justify it to the voters if it is concerned with its vote position.

The presence of isolation in public goods carries the implication of learned utility, both before and after the fact of purchase. The greater the degree of isolation, the greater the degree to which utility can be affected by influence production on the part of external agents. Because of this there will be less "self-correction" in the public market than there was in the private. Consumers are less able to determine actual utility from experience and then to alter estimations of future utility on the basis of this experience.

Thus, even accepting Downs' analysis of voter behavior, there are serious difficulties presented in our positive model. Voters not only are uncertain as to the effects of government action on their utility, they often do not even have their utility functions formulated until after government action has been taken. Utility derived from public goods is in large measure endogenous and voting behavior is therefore not independent of influence.

Non-Voting Influence. Consumers are affected by the actions of the government and on occasion they have an intense interest in the outcome of a policy decision. This will most often be the case with regard to public actions in which the degree of isolation is very low for particular consumers or groups of consumers, e.g., farmers who are directly affected by price supports. These interested consumers will generally stand to gain or lose substantial amounts depending on the decision made, and as a result will have strong preferences with respect to these government actions.

Voting, however, does not really permit a means of evaluating consumer preferences as we saw in Part I. Furthermore, in a system of representative government, there is really no way in which consumers can express preferences on any single issue through the election process. Voters cast their ballots for an individual who must take any number of positions on any number of issues. The election of a candidate or party may be regarded as an expression of overall approval for the programs of that party, but it cannot be regarded as an expression of preferences with regard to any one issue.

As a result, those individuals and groups with an especially strong interest in one particular issue will have to use non-voting methods of expressing their preferences. In fact, governmental decisions, once the government has been elected, will be almost exclusively the result of non-voting influence. This topic is of such great importance that we devote an entire section of the book, Part IV, to a discussion of it.

There are two general forms that non-voting influence produced by consumers can take: that which provides information as to preferences, and that which provides resources for influence of voter utility. In the first case, influence revolves around the fact that government must maximize votes to maintain office. Many votes will be necessary to accomplish this and votes are dependent upon consumer utility. Hence governments must be aware of consumers preferences or they must alter them to fit programs instituted if they are to be successful; but governments, like everyone else in our system, suffer from a high degree of uncertainty.

Interested individuals may take advantage of this by providing government with selective information on the intensity of consumer preferences. This subsidization of information acquisition may take the form of letter-writing campaigns, direct lobbying with the legislature, demonstrations or newspaper ads. To the extent government is susceptible to influence, its decisions will be altered by this type of activity.

The second form which influence may assume centers around the need of government for real resources with which to finance its campaigns. Voters' utility functions are partially learned in the process of acquiring subsidized information, but this process of subsidization requires the investment of real resources on the part of the influencer. Governments can acquire some of these resources by taxation but the rest must come from owners of real resources. These owners, if they are going to remain in our system, will be operating in their self-interest and will trade these resources to those parties that propose the most beneficial programs. These need not be an explicit trade; as we shall see in Part IV, it may be almost unnoticeable.

Any interested group could utilize any or all of these methods of non-voting influence to attempt to affect the decisions of government. The method actually chosen may often be a function of the position of the interested party in the income distribution.[12] We could separate techniques of producing influence into money-intensive and time-intensive methods and argue that relatively poor groups with a relative abundance of time and manpower will use time-intensive methods such as demonstrations. On the other hand, groups with a relatively high endowment of income and wealth may be expected to engage in resource intense methods of influence such as contributing to campaigns and hiring lobbyists. To the extent that the attempts of these interest groups are effective, government decisions will reflect not the will of the majority, but the will of the most intensely interested minority.

Consumers and the Bureaucracy. There is another branch of the public sector in our model, the bureaucracy, and groups of consumers have direct contacts with this branch. For the most part, the consumers who will be most interested in the operation of any particular bureau are the ones that make up its clientele. They may attempt to affect the actions of this bureau, but the form in which this is most often seen is the use of non-voting influence exerted on government. Thus, welfare recipients may demonstrate in front of the legislature to get better treatment from case workers. The bureaucrats themselves are not subject to direct voter approval but only indirect approval. Consumers who recognize this fact will use the medium of the government as a tool to alter bureaucratic policies, if the incentive for doing so is greater than the costs of creating influence.

CONCLUSIONS

Consumer behavior in both the private and public sectors is based upon a desire to maximize utility. In the private sector this involves the trade of money for real goods and services; in the public it involves the trade of votes as an expression of preferences and the use of non-voting means of influence to affect public decisions. The consumers of our model differ from more traditional consumers, however, in that their preferences are no longer given. By assuming that utility functions are stable and internally generated, the standard analysis is eliminating a large portion of the economic process through which the allocation of

---

[12] I am indebted to Prof. R. Coen for first making this observation in a conversation.

resources is determined. Even a cursory examination of the precepts of the other social sciences leads to the conclusion that large scale values, and even the values placed upon specific goods, are learned from the social environment.

If values are learned, and if this learning process can be manipulated to reach a desired end, then rational economic agents must attempt to influence the formation of utility and hence behavior of other agents whenever their expected gain exceeds the cost of producing influence. This process is evident in the private market in the determination of demand for products. Because of the increased isolation in the operation of the public sector, the process is especially prevalent there.

It is important to note that we make no normative judgments regarding the process of influencing preferences, and indeed we can make none without some external, absolute standard. If all values are learned, we cannot say that those learned from one source are in any respect better than those learned from another source. If we admit that preferences can be and, indeed, have been altered over time, then to allocate resources in the present on the basis of past preferences would represent a misallocation of resources in the accepted definition of the term.

Only in the case where an intentional divergence has been introduced between expected and actual utility to the extent that consumers' actual utility streams have been diminished can we make any judgments, and we can do so here only if actual utility is not subsequently altered so that it coincides with expected.

To say that preferences do not change over time is to ignore reality; to assume that these changes are not in part caused by external agents and events is in a sense to assume irrationality on the part of those who could benefit through influence. Uncertainty is at the heart of this influencing process and it is this uncertainty and the costs of reaching collective decisions that require the delegation of public purchasing decisions to representatives through a process which effectively insulates these decisions from consumer preferences.

CHAPTER 4
GOVERNMENT
BEHAVIOR

You do not know, and the worst of it is, since the responsibility is mine, I do not know what they [voters] are thinking about. I have the most imperfect means of finding out, and yet I have to act as if I knew.

Woodrow Wilson

[The isolation of high office] . . . is inevitable. Not only physical isolation, but you're isolated by a kind of network. You're kind of surrounded by a political environment. Your political education is directed toward one purpose—supporting Administration decisions. . . . Every morning you start with those reports. From Security, C.I.A., State, Defense. And they're all full of information that buttresses a decision that's already been made. All that secret data in support of the policy that's already been made.

Hubert H. Humphrey

I cannot recall any project of any size that has ever been presented to this committee that came out in the end like the witnesses said it would at the outset.

Representative Prince Preston

Governments demonstrate a great variability of forms, both in theory and in practice. We can conceive of governments which are nearly anarchic or we can imagine ones which are based upon absolute totalitarianism. The form which a government in the real world assumes will have implications for the operations of the relevant society in which it exists. But no matter where along the political spectrum it is located, it will have to act in an environment of great uncertainty. As a result government behavior will always reflect two important facts: first, governments cannot know for certain what they should do, and secondly, they cannot know for certain what they are doing.

We have postulated a democratic, or at least a republican form of governmental organization in our model, but much of the behavior outlined could be found in other systems. For the sake of simplicity we shall assume that there is a single body of government which is responsible for the formation and enforcement of laws. This releases us from explicit consideration of relationships between state, local, and federal forms of government—we need only deal with a single, national level government with jurisdiction over all collective activity. This government is to be composed of a number of individuals, each of whom is subject to election by consumers. Each serves a fixed term of office and then must be approved by the electorate if he is to continue to hold his position. Groups of candidates may try to take advantage of economies of scale in electioneering by combining into "political parties" rather than running as independents.[1]

We shall further assume that the winner of any election is that candidate, or group of candidates in a "party" election, who receives a majority of the votes cast. Rational behavior in our model certainly includes the possibility of abstention on the part of many voters, and hence their preferences are not important in the selection of the group of candidates which will make up the government. Once elected, the members of the government are assumed to operate without fear of instantaneous voter rejection, save in the case of gross misconduct sufficient to justify recall or impeachment. In all other instances voters may remove a government or specific members of it only on the specified dates of elections through the normal voting process.

We assume, in addition, that each voter has a single vote for each office, and that there is no "point voting" or other similar institution. Moreover, in our model there is no legal means of explicitly buying or selling votes. Each individual must cast his own ballot or let it go unused.

GOVERNMENTAL DECISION MAKING

The decisions which a government makes will be based upon the government's view of consumers' preference functions. It will be attempting to maximize its vote position, and hence will undertake those projects which it thinks will yield a net increase in votes and will reject all others. The use of this principle in practice is made extremely difficult because of the presence, once again, of gross uncertainty.[2] There are

---

[1] Cf. Downs, *op. cit.* He uses parties rather than candidates as his political units and he discusses the advantages of party organization.

[2] Even a world of certainty does not insure the predominance of majority rule. If representatives in government are responsible to different constituencies, then with equal representation, $\frac{1}{2} + 1$ members of $\frac{1}{2} + 1$ of the constituencies

two distinct aspects of this uncertainty as it affects government's interaction with consumers.

The first of these stems from the ineffectiveness of voting for representatives as an expression of preferences with regard to particular issues. The government is largely unaware of what consumers wish, and hence it runs the risk of losing votes by taking the "wrong" action. In its attempts to eliminate this risk, it will acquire a certain amount of information as to voters' preferences and the relative intensity with which they regard particular issues and outcomes. Like all rational agents, the government is susceptible to influence in the form of subsidized information which relates to this problem. On the other side, those with a strong incentive to produce influence and the means with which to finance the subsidization will take advantage of this susceptibility on the part of government.

This influence may take the form of providing government directly with information as to the intensity of consumer preferences, e.g., it may consist of large demonstrations, the presentation of petitions, massive correspondence campaigns stressing particular issues, the purchase of newspaper space or television time, etc. In this situation, either consumers or producers may see the opportunity for gain. Government also acquires a certain amount of information as to preferences through public hearings and the informational gathering proceedings of committees. Interested individuals may see an opportunity to provide selective information in this manner as well.

Consumers or producers, or for that matter bureaucrats, may also use information to affect indirectly government's decisions. Not only is government often unaware of the nature of consumer preferences, it is also unaware of all of the ramifications of its actions on utility producing phenomena. For example, not only does the purchase of a new highway system affect the ability of consumers to move from one area to another, the program of construction will have an effect upon the employment rate in different areas of the country. Individuals may provide government with information as to these secondary effects which in turn may influence government to undertake a particular purchase which on its own merits is not justified in the preliminary esti-

---

can determine the outcome, i.e., slightly more than 1/4 of the voters constitute a "majority." If the voters are distributed unevenly among the various representatives, then it is possible for less than 1/4 of the total number of voters to be decisive on any one issue.

Charles Schultze also stresses this fact and the whole process of delegating decision power to the bureaucracy that results from it.

> [The] . . . most important reason for the increasing military budget is the fact that some of the most fundamental decisions that determine their size are seldom subjected to outside review and only occasionally discussed and debated in the public arena.[5]

Government is simply not able to be aware of what it is actually purchasing in most cases. It has to depend upon the bureaucracy to handle most of its affairs. To the extent that the bureaucracy, or parts of it, have an interest in the outcome of public purchasing decisions, it will be able to take advantage of governmental uncertainty to produce influence. This influence will consist of information which reinforces decisions made on the lower level of the bureaucracy, along with an increase in the price of information which contradicts its decisions.

CONCLUSIONS

Government actions that affect public purchases take place in an environment of uncertainty. Theoretically government should weigh the alternative purchasing programs and then choose the one which provides the greatest increase in consumer utility. Realistically, government is unable to determine what consumers' preferences are, nor is it really able to evaluate and be aware of what it is buying. In such a situation interested agents will see an opportunity to gain by influencing the process of collective choice. The outcome of the purchasing decisions will depend upon the manner in which the uncertainty of the government is reduced. By providing selective, subsidized information those agents with a strong enough incentive, and also sufficient means to produce influence, will affect the decisions that the government makes. In many cases these decisions will reflect the desires of the most intensely interested minorities rather than the will of the majority.

Once made, the government must then provide consumers with information which is designed to increase their perceived utility from the purchasing program. All decisions made by the vote-maximizing collective body must either be obscured or justified. However, the actual process of voting has very little to do with public choice; it is almost exclusively the result of non-voting influence and pressures.

[5] Charles Schultze, "Re-examining the Military Budget," in *The Public Interest*, Winter 1970, p. 17.

CHAPTER 5
PRODUCER
BEHAVIOR

In normative theory, the purchasing decisions of government are aimed exclusively at increasing the utility of consumers. Producers enter the picture after the decisions have been made and act only in response to an increase in the demand for particular products that are now desired by consumers acting collectively. The behavior of producers in this regard is no different than in the private sector under an assumption of consumer sovereignty. In both cases the role of producers is largely a passive one of responding to consumer demands rather than stimulating them. In our positive model, such behavior on the part of the producers would be irrational, for now the pervading atmosphere is one of uncertainty where there is the potential for influencing the demand curves faced by each firm. To leave this potential untapped would imply irrationality on the part of producers; they have an option for an improvement in their situation and they must take advantage of it. Any time they can realize a net increase in their profits by influencing the behavior of other individuals in the system, they will do so. In the system we have set up we can observe this process of influence in both the private and public sectors.

PRODUCERS IN THE PRIVATE MARKET

The altered view of utility which was developed in the section on consumer behavior carries implications for producers as well. The demand curves which they face are no longer fixed, but are subject to change as a direct result of action taken by the firm. This may be a short term change as expected utility is made to diverge from actual utility, or the effects may be of longer duration if the firm is able to create a new need or alter the perceived characteristics of its product. Both of these situations were outlined in some detail earlier. All that is necessary before this process takes place is that the firm believe that the increase in revenues from influence will exceed the sum of the costs of influence and the additional costs of production.

PRODUCERS IN THE PUBLIC MARKET

For some firms, a large share of their output is not purchased by individual consumers but is sold instead to all consumers collectively. These are the firms who sell to the government, and the demand curves they face are the result of consumer utility only to the extent that government action is a result of it. To the extent that government purchasing decisions are made on the basis of non-voting influence and pressures, the demand curves these firms face will be a result of such influence. In this situation, rational firms will participate in the influencing of government decisions in an attempt to alter these curves in a way which is favorable to their profit situation. Firms are supposed to merely respond to demand, but particularly in the public arena we can witness them actively trying to create demand. There are several reasons why such activity is especially profitable in the case of public goods.

One of these stems from the fact that it is possible to influence the purchases of a large number of consumers by influencing only a very small number of decision makers. There is a dichotomy between those who buy, consumers, and those who decide to buy, government, in our model. By creating influence which affects those who decide to buy, it is possible to affect the purchases of a large number of consumers without really creating any change in consumers' utility.[1] The form which this influence will take may be based upon either the direct subsidization of information acquired by government or it may involve the trade of resources for favorable purchasing decisions. This type of demand creation is particularly appealing to producers because of the isolation involved in the purchase of public goods. In many cases consumers will not even know that they have bought the good in question to say nothing of being unable to adequately evaluate the need for, and quality of, particular items. There will, therefore, be less of a chance of the self-correction process of the private market reversing the purchasing patterns created by producer influence.

---

[1] This type of situation is not found exclusively in the realm of public goods. Anytime consumers rely on the advice of "experts" when making purchasing decisions, producers can benefit by influencing the experts rather than the consumers. Witness, for example, the extensive expenditures made by drug companies to entertain and ostensibly enlighten doctors as to the properties of particular drugs. To the extent that they can influence doctors, or sufficiently entertain them, the companies will be affecting the purchases made by patients of the doctors rather than the doctors themselves.

We can also see an advantage accruing to producers of public goods in that they can be certain of very little countering influence being produced by consumer interests. This is because of the strong asymmetry between the relative costs and benefits which the two groups may expect. The potential gain to a producer from raising his demand curve is relatively high, while his costs of causing this shift of demand are relatively low in the public arena for the reasons outlined above. For the consumer, however, his share of the costs of the increased purchases will probably be a rather small proportion of his total income and expenditures while his expected costs of becoming informed about public purchases are quite high and his costs of individually altering them nearly astronomical. As a result, most producer-created influence relating to the public purchasing decision will not be counterbalanced by pressure from consumers.

A final impact of producers' entry into the determination of public policy may be found in the area of restricting competition. Nearly all analysts of market systems recognize the presence of market imperfections that limit competition in the sale and production of specific goods. Government is generally charged with the responsibility of enforcing competition in those markets where it would otherwise be restricted. In our model, the actions of government may indeed serve to restrict competition rather than enforce it. Government has no interest in competition per se; it is driven by a desire to maximize votes. Whenever it feels that its vote position will be improved by reducing rather than increasing the competition in particular markets, it will do so. This will be easier to do when it can provide some justification to the voters for its actions.

An example of this is the Mandatory Oil Import Control Program which effectively restricts foreign competition in the sale of oil within the United States. According to *Business Week,* this program cost American consumers approximately $6.2 billion in 1969 by arbitrarily raising the price of crude oil some $1.25 per barrel.[2] The government provides a justification for this program by claiming that it is necessary for national defense to develop oil fields at home. (One might ask if it wouldn't be wiser to use foreign oil while shipping lanes are open and save our domestic deposits for times of war when transport is hazardous.)

[2] *Business Week,* August 30, 1969, p. 96.

Indeed, it is the thesis of Walter Adams and H. M. Gray that monopolies do not often arise out of the interplay of market forces, but instead they are more often the direct result of government restrictions on the competition within a particular market.[3] Adams claims that the high level of industrial concentration found in the U. S. today is not a result of technological change, but stems instead from "unwise, man-made, discriminatory, privilege-creating governmental action."[4]

Government in our system would engage in such action under one of two situations: either it felt, on the basis of the information at hand, that restricting competition would increase votes because of secondary effects upon employment, price stability, etc., or alternatively, if it felt that such action would produce large amounts of resources with which to finance the process of influencing voter behavior. Producers in our model would use either approach if they felt that they could increase net profits by such an undertaking.

Producers also interact in the public sector with the bureaucracy. As we have seen, most purchasing decisions are actually initiated within the bureaucracy and are then passed upward and consolidated into large packages which are then approved or rejected by the government. As a result, many of producers' actions aimed at increasing effective demand for their products will take place in relations with bureaucrats rather than members of government. There is a unique market situation when bureaucrats and producers discuss purchases that is not like any other in a market system. We shall postpone a complete discussion of this situation until we outline the behavior of the bureaucracy in the next chapter. It is sufficient to state for the moment that the outcome is not identical to that in the producer-consumer interaction.

CONCLUSIONS

While producers are supposed to respond to given demand patterns, in reality the demand facing producers is at least partially endogenous. As a result, their desire to maximize profits requires them to engage in activities explicitly aimed at altering the demand they face. This activ-

---

[3] Walter Adams and H. M. Gray, *Monopoly in America: The Government as Promoter*, New York, 1955.
[4] Walter Adams, "The Military-Industrial Complex and the New Industrial State," *A.E.A. Papers and Proceedings*, Vol. LVII, May 1968, pp. 652–665, p. 653.

ity will be present in both the private and public sectors, but for several reasons, it will be more prevalent in the latter. Here the potential gain is increased because of the reduced number of individuals who must be influenced, the isolation of products from consumers, and the uncertainty of government as to what it should buy as well as what it is buying. The uncertainty which is most important for producers is that which surrounds those with whom they deal. By selectively reducing this uncertainty or by providing resources which government can in turn use to influence voters, producers can enter the process of public decision making as active participants. Indeed, in most purchasing decisions producers will play a far more active role than will consumers, and the outcome of these decisions will reflect the asymmetry. Producers can no longer be regarded as merely responding to the desires of other agents.

CHAPTER 6
BUREAUCRATIC
BEHAVIOR

It is not so much the inefficiency of bureaucracy we complain about as its efficiency for purposes other than those we feel appropriate.

Robert Wood

In our model we have defined the bureaucracy as the permanent component of the public sector, responsible to the government for its actions but not subject to direct voter approval. Members of the bureaucracy do not serve fixed terms of office, but instead hold their positions indefinitely. They handle the collection, analysis, and sorting of information for the government and pass their conclusions on for approval. They also handle the day-to-day administration of much of the government's activity in the public sector. To be sure, the distinction between bureaucrats and members of the government becomes rather tenuous at the highest levels in most real world societies, but we shall draw an arbitrary line between those who are elected and those who are not for the sake of analysis.

In Part I we discussed the implications of self-interest for the behavior of bureaucrats, and concluded that they would be motivated by a desire to maximize bureaucratic security. Since the most visible measure of the strength of a bureau is the size and rate of growth of its budget, the drive for security will be reflected in a desire to insure continual reinforcement of this measure. This will have implications for the behavior of bureaucrats in their relationships with the other central groups in our positive system. Let us turn now to an examination of these implications.

GOVERNMENT AND THE BUREAUCRACY

In the section on government behavior above, we stressed the fact that budgetary decisions are really initiated within the bureaucracy and are then consolidated and finally passed on to the government for review and approval. Because of government's high degree of uncertainty and the costs it would have to incur in order to eliminate this uncertainty, rationality requires it to rely on the acquisition of information provided by the bureaucracy at reduced cost. The bureaucracy, in its pursuit of security, will provide selective information to the government which reinforces the decisions it has made at a lower level. These decisions will reflect a desire to find as many "justifiable" and "essential" expenditures as possible.

There are, of course, some limits on the bureaucracy's ability to do this, and the bureaucrats are aware of them. Their security depends on striking a balance between increased expenditures and avoiding a too careful review of these expenditures. Governments, who must react to consumer preferences when they are aware of them, will investigate carefully any programs which become so large that they are obvious. Similarly, they will examine programs which exhibit unusually large increases from one period to the next. Whenever bureaucratic actions cause large-scale, noticeable changes from the point of view of government or consumers, then government will have to discount much of the information provided by the bureaus and incur the costs of acquiring nonsubsidized information. This is necessitated by its concern over its vote position.

Within the confines of this limit, the bureaucracy may be able to artificially increase its expenses. This occurs not only for the bureaucracy as a whole, but also within each individual agency. The individuals at the top of each large department are as much subject to influence in the need for funds as the members of government.

The role of administration of purchasing decisions allows bureaucrats another tool for influencing governmental decisions. By trading expenditures favorable to particular members of the government for their support of budget measures, bureaucrats may have an influence. For example, the bureau in charge of letting government contracts for space equipment may award it to firms in the districts of particular Congressmen in exchange for their support of the space program. The resulting increase in employment and profits within this district can be used to increase or at least reinforce the vote position of the Congressman. Similarly, the higher level of profits may induce the affected firms to contribute resources to assist in the influence of voter behavior in the next election.

There is once again a limit to this process, for if the trading becomes too blatant, there is the possibility for sufficient public distrust to undermine this advantage.[1] Nevertheless, through the use of information and its purchasing power the bureaucracy will influence government decisions with an eye toward increasing its security rather than consumers' utility.

Its ability to do this will be greatest in those purchases where the degree of isolation from consumers is greatest and where the technical complexity of the items in question is greatest. In these cases the ability of consumers to evaluate the utility to be derived from their purchases in the public sector is smallest and they are most dependent upon subsidized information. As a result, the vote position of government is less jeopardized by unnecessary purchases of this type. For example, an increase in expenditures for missile systems can more easily be influenced than can an increase of the same amount in expenditures for sewage systems. Consumers' estimations of the former are largely subject to externally provided information; the need for sewers is more readily apparent to the layman.

As a result of this, bureaucrats will be able to induce government to approve many purchases whose sole real contribution is the enhancement of the position of the bureaucracy and its members rather than the utility of consumers. As long as the changes in purchasing patterns are marginal in terms of size and as long as they are sufficiently isolated from consumers, these purchases will not be subject to any self-correction process. This tendency of bureaucrats to overspend is often reinforced by the irrationality of economizing on expenditures. In practice, all of an appropriation must be spent or the allocation of funds to the particular bureau in question will be reduced in the next period. Hence, if an agency finds itself with excess funds after meeting its initially planned expenses, it is rational for it to find some other justifiable, or at least relatively invisible, use for the funds.

CONSUMERS AND THE BUREAUCRACY

Consumers form the effective limit on bureaucratic actions through a two-step process. They have no direct control over it, but they have some control over government through voting and non-voting means

---

[1] Apparently, in some cases, even this is not an important consideration. Many congressmen openly campaign on a record of increased defense contracts for their particular district and an unquestioning attitude toward increased budget demands of the defense department. It is important to note that these increases may not appear at all "artificial" to the bureaucrats involved. "Artificiality" in this

of influence and thus they can affect the bureaucracy. The current trend toward reductions in defense spending is largely the result of Congressional awareness that voters' utility is being adversely affected by the size of that budget. (The change in voters' utility is probably largely the result of changes in their stock of information and an alteration of their discount factors.) Bureaucrats who recognize the necessity of appearing beneficial to consumers will utilize selective information to present a favorable picture of their actions and effectiveness. Very few bureaucratic publications indeed provide information as to how the publishing agency has wasted funds, engaged in superfluous activities, and reduced consumer utility. On the contrary, they almost universally stress the contributions made and the necessity for increasing the resources allocated to the agency in question.[2]

At the same time these agencies will attempt to raise the relative price of information unfavorable to the expansion of their budgets. On occasion the efforts made to do this will be extreme and the penalties visited upon those who violate this norm will be most severe. It matters not whether the information would increase voters' utility or the ability of government to make accurate decisions, if it is detrimental to the attainment of bureaucratic security it will be suppressed.[3]

---

case is with respect to consumers desires. Bureaucrats may find any number of "important" and "useful" ways to spend consumers' income that consumers nevertheless would not approve of if they were aware of them.

[2] This drive for security may be carried to the extreme levels where bureaus would be exhibiting irrational behavior if they actually operated efficiently in the manner they are "supposed" to operate. Many agencies are aimed at handling a particular problem, but if the problem is actually solved, or at least reduced in intensity there is no longer any need for the agency to exist at such high levels. For example, the successful culmination of the war on poverty means an end not only to hunger, but also to O.E.O., etc. For antipoverty agencies to be too efficient is to be "suicidal."

[3] Witness, for example, the case of Ernest Fitzgerald as described in *Newsweek,* November 17, 1969, pp. 106–108. Mr. Fitzgerald worked as a cost analyst in the Pentagon and freely provided a Congressional subcommittee with information detrimental to the Defense Department. He testified that the C-5A would probably run over its budget of $3.2 billion dollars by some $2 billion. Twelve days later he was informed that it was "computer error" that had informed him of his permanent appointment prior to the testimony. He was then told that he was no longer needed at meetings regarding major weapons systems and given his new assignment—an analysis of costs at a bowling alley in Thailand. As if this weren't enough, for disclosing a waste of $2 billion, he was fired in an economy move and his functions were fulfilled by John Dyment, a $107.92 a day consultant with Arthur Young and Co., which also handles the accounting for Lockheed Aircraft, the producer of the C-5A. Highly irrational behavior for a "machine" maximizing collective utility; quite predictable for one maximizing its own security.

PRODUCERS AND THE BUREAUCRACY

The funds which government allocates to the bureaucracy are in turn traded to producers for real goods and services in a series of market transactions. However, the nature of these transactions differs from any others found in our economic system because of the unusual motivations of the two participating groups. Normally, transactions take place between consumers who are attempting to get the most possible value for their money by keeping prices low and producers who are attempting to get the most money possible for their goods by keeping prices high. The conflicting goals of the two agents place limitations on the solution of the market problem which are not found in this new situation.

In this case we have producers still attempting to sell their goods at the highest possible price trading with bureaucrats who may be more concerned with spending than with what they are getting for their money. The constraints present in normal market situations do not apply here. These transactions are not totally unconstrained, however, because governments must still answer to the voters and bureaucrats in turn must answer to the government. Still, we have seen that governments suffer from a relatively high degree of uncertainty as to the nature and efficiency of bureaucratic actions and unless agencies become blatant in their misuse of information it will rely on bureaucratic evaluations of bureaucratic actions.

The actual purchase of public goods then takes place between producers and members of the bureaucracy, neither one of which has any real direct interest in either low prices or consumer utility. There is no reason to assume that the outcome of the decision will be optimal from the standpoint of either of these criteria, or even to assume that they entered into the decision at all. Murray Weidenbaum claims that only 10% to 12% of the total value of military procurement is made on the basis of sealed bidding for the lowest price. The rest is made on the basis of negotiated settlements between producers of military goods and agents of the Defense Department.[4]

Within certain limits then the rational pursuit of their respective goals requires both bureaus and the producers of public goods to desire high levels of spending, not on the basis of consumer utility but

[4] Murray Weidenbaum, *The Military Market in the United States,* American Marketing Association, 1963, p. 30.

for their own self-interest. This tendency is further aggravated by the budget practice of penalizing thrift discussed above. If a bureau finds itself accomplishing its specified tasks with funds left over, it will be rational for it to search actively for an outlet for the excess, and, if possible, for means of creating a "healthy" overrun. It will be rational for profit maximizing producers of publicly purchased goods to provide assistance in this search.

CONCLUSIONS

A majority of all public purchasing decisions are born not in the minds of consumers or even politicians, but in the interaction of producers and bureaucrats. Politicians and voters may discuss "national priorities" and "missile gaps" but such things are not purchased in the market. Governments purchase not "defense" and "education" but steel, bullets, desks, and books. The decision to acquire these items is made in a market bounded by producers and bureaucrats, both of whom have an interest in finding expenses which can be either hidden, or justified to the government and, if necessary, to the voters. The decision, once made, will be passed upward through the bureaucratic ranks with a good deal of selective information designed to create a favorable atmosphere until the government finally votes on an aggregated budget with almost no knowledge of the actual purchases it contains. Consumer preferences are at least two steps away from this purchase decision and there is no rational way of bringing them closer in the face of such gross uncertainty.

Bureaucrats make purchasing decisions and the goal which underlies the decisions is the maximization of security. The two sectors with which the bureaucracy has the closest contact are the profit maximizing producers and the vote maximizing government—it has minimal contact with consumers and almost no awareness of their utility functions.

CHAPTER 7
THE SYSTEM
AS A WHOLE

Much like Frankenstein's monster, the subject when put back together bears little resemblance to its predecessors from which many of its parts were taken. There have been three significant alterations in the physiology of the system, and as a result of these we can predict a number of behavioral abnormalities as viewed by the standards of health derived from earlier models. In brief, the three major changes are:

1. Consumers' utility functions upon which they base their actions in both the private and public sectors are no longer fixed and given. They are at least partially endogenous and the behavior of consumers can be affected by conscious attempts at influencing them.
2. The government, which is charged with the responsibility of reaching collective decisions, exists in a sea of vast uncertainty. It neither knows for sure what it should do, nor in fact what it is doing in many cases. Where government comes to shore in the public purchasing decision is largely dependent upon how this uncertainty is reduced, i.e., upon who pushes hardest and in what direction.
3. The actual acquisition of goods and services takes place in a unique market situation. The "antagonists" in this trade are not particularly concerned with low prices or consumers' utility—they have other concerns of greater importance to them and it is these which are reflected in public purchasing choices. Government merely approves or disapproves the outcome of this market interaction. Even though it has responsibilty for public purchases, it seldom participates in them.

These changes lead us to a few conclusions regarding the outcome of the public purchasing decision which are of some importance.

First, in a normal model the patterns of final demand for the economy as a whole are the result of consumers' preferences. These may be expressed in the private market or in the public sector. In our model, a large segment of this pattern will not be dependent upon consumer utility as such, but will be the direct result of influence and pressure. These demands will tend to favor most heavily those agents with a high monetary incentive to influence the decision, and sufficient resources and organization to finance the production of this influence. This implies that much of the pattern of demand in the public sector will be aimed at furthering producers' goals rather than consumers', since the incentive is greater for producers with regard to any one issue. Consumer sovereignty suffers a serious decrease in its real power in our system as a result.

Similarly, there will be a strong tendency to maintain the status quo in public purchases since the costs of changes will be quite real and quite apparent to producers of goods now purchased. Their incentive to influence decisions is very high and because of information already in the hands of deciders and established contacts, their costs are relatively low. Agents attempting to alter the established pattern have less certain gains to expect, higher costs of influence since they must overcome the effects of existing stocks of information, and finally, they have to establish new contacts. Once again producers will have the strongest incentive for influence, and an established producer will normally only be "deposed" by another producer rather than by consumers' actions. Patterns once established are on firm ground; significant changes face many obstacles.

Second, the allocation of resources which results in a system such as the one described in our model will not be Pareto optimal for a number of reasons.

1. Even if all influence completely canceled out so that no distortions of any kind were introduced into the system and all agents' actions were the same as if they were completely independent, all of the resources used to produce influence will have been wasted. They could have been used in the production of utility yielding goods, and hence they represent an unrealized potential increase in utility.

2. Because all consumers purchase all public goods, and because they really are not able to significantly influence the choice to purchase them, some individuals will be buying quantities that are either too large or too small from their point of view.

3. The peculiar market situation between bureaucrats and producers implies that purchase decisions will be made without explicit refer-

ence to price or consumer desires. As a result there is no reason to expect these decisions to reflect consumers' marginal rates of substitution.

4. Because of (3) the payments to factors of production will not be indicative of consumers' demands, and hence the incomes of those agents controlling resources used in public production will be "artificially" raised. This will have repercussions back onto the allocation of resources in the private market as they will shift into positions which reflect the higher incomes and wants of these agents.

5. Because of producers' extra incentive to influence purchases which is not countered by consumers' incentives to do so, there may be a tendency to over-purchase public goods in general compared with a situation of certainty. There will definitely be a tendency to over-purchase some items, particularly those which exhibit the highest degrees of isolation.

6. Finally, the attainment of Pareto optimality will be inhibited by the tendency of government to restrict rather than enforce competition whenever it is convinced that such action will favorably affect its vote position. Competition per se has no appeal to government.

Finally, we can conclude that although Pareto optimality is un-attainable within this system, it is not at all clear what this implies since Pareto optimality has lost its meaning. Normally, the concept of Pareto optimality begins with a set of fixed preference functions, production functions, and resource endowments and claims that an optimal situation exists whenever the marginal rates of substitution in production and consumption have been equated to the relative price ratios for each pair of goods and each consumer. In our model, utility functions have become endogenous and this concept of optimality is no longer applicable. An individual who contributes to the purchase of a good in the public sector and learns to attach a positive utility to it only after the purchase does not fit the formula for Pareto optimality. Utility functions altered to fit established patterns of consumption destroy the meaning of the concept. Another criteria for judging the operations of a positive system must be devised, or alternatively, such judgments must be delegated to the realm of the subjective. Paretian criteria do not work.

These conclusions present a negative picture of the world which is perhaps unpleasing. The allocation of resources to the production of those goods and services which consumers most desire cannot progress efficiently in the absence of a public sector. This was made clear in Part I. However, in the presence of a public sector it is now clear that this allocation cannot progress efficiently. The world is an imperfect place, and the systems which operate in it suffer this same fate of imperfection. This is not the result of evil conspiracies or radical alterations in the assumed nature of the agents in an economic system. Yet we must conclude that when we turn our self-interested, rational individuals loose in a world of uncertainty their behavior will impart a degree of partial paralysis to Adam Smith's famed invisible hand.

PART

III

POSITIVE
PRINCIPLES
OF
TAXATION

INTRODUCTION

> The struggle to overcome arbitrariness in taxation was one of the early objectives of constitutional government; and the setting of tax maxims provided a means of defining the status of the individual in the social compact.
>
> Richard Musgrave

By its very nature the intervention of the government into the economic process is a two-sided coin, yet the two sides are not necessarily in close proximity at all times. The act of purchase implicitly assumes a corresponding act of taxation in order to raise the required funds. On occasion, government purchases will entail the issuance of new money rather than direct taxation, but even in this case the extensive use of money creation will levy an indirect "inflation tax" on the holders of money balances. Any time the government utilizes resources in the public sector, some agent must forego their use in the private sector.

The peculiarity of this situation lies in the fact that the one to one correspondence of cost to benefit found in private market transactions is not necessarily present in public purchases. The act of purchasing is effectively isolated from the act of acquiring revenues. The decision to tax is effectively isolated from the decision to buy public goods. In Part II we examined the process of making public purchasing decisions and the influences made on these decisions in an uncertain world. In Part III we shall examine the process of determining the tax structure in a positive model, and the means by which different groups attempt to shift the incidence of taxes onto other individuals and groups.

NORMATIVE PRINCIPLES

The normative literature on taxation centers its discussions around two basic principles to be used in determining tax burdens, the "benefit" approach and the "ability-to-pay" approach.[1] The benefit principle states that taxes should be levied upon those individuals who gain from the program of public expense and in proportion to their gain. It is re-

---

[1] Cf. Richard Musgrave, The Theory of Public Finance, MaGraw-Hill, New York, 1959, especially Chapters 4 and 5.

garded as an "efficient" means of determining tax burdens since it allows, and in fact requires, a simultaneous determination of both expenditures and taxes. It thus follows in the spirit of free exchange which theoretically pervades private markets.

The ability-to-pay principle argues that taxes should be distributed in a manner which equalizes the utility sacrifice required of all tax payers, i.e., they are taxed in accordance with their income or wealth. This is regarded as an "equitable" means of tax distribution since it is supposed to provide for a relatively "just" solution.

In practice, we find some rather severe difficulties in using either of these principles; first, because the realities of an uncertain world make the administration of taxes on either principle grossly unfeasible and secondly, because there is no reason to assume that the use of these normative principles would lead to a vote maximizing position for the government. Government in our model is motivated by a desire to retain office, and it will distribute the tax burden with this in mind. If potential methods of distribution do not contribute to this end, government will not use them no matter how great their normative desirability. Equity and efficiency take second place to votes.

In order for a benefit principle to be feasible as a basis for a tax structure, it would be necessary to have an accurate means of finding and aggregating individual's preferences, and an institutional arrangement that allowed an efficient expression of these preferences for each individual purchasing decision. Unfortunately, we have found both of these conditions to be unsatisfied in our earlier analysis. The first requirement would be necessary to guage the benefit accruing to each individual voter in order to allocate costs accordingly, but we saw that it is irrational to express these preferences. As a result, voting does not allow a means of determining appropriate tax burdens. The second requirement stems from the fact that it would be necessary to know the utility derived from individual projects if consumers' real benefits were to be gauged. Earmarked taxes for each purchase distributed among consumers would be the best solution to the "benefit" problem since this most closely approximates the idea of voluntary exchange. We have seen that this is not feasible either, since the costs of reaching collective decisions make it rational to delegate authority to small numbers of individuals who make all small decisions without real knowledge of consumers' utility functions. In terms of institutional arrangements this implies that wide-scale voting, even if it were an accurate means of discovering preferences, would not be a rational approach to public decision making because of the excessive costs involved.

Moreover, even if it were used, voters would not be able to vote from an informed position because the costs of becoming informed would generally exceed any expected benefit. The rationality of concealing preferences for public goods and the necessity of delegating public choice to representatives because of decision making costs combine to destroy any real possibility of utilizing a benefit approach effectively in the determination of tax burdens.

The "ability-to-pay" approach suffers much the same fate as the "benefit" approach in terms of its chances of survival in a realistic situation. Even in purely theoretical terms there are certain obvious difficulties in using this principle. For example, it is not at all clear how we should define "ability-to-pay" since it necessarily involves the cardinal crime of welfare economics, making interpersonal utility comparisons. There is no truly objective way of doing this. Moreover, it would require making a decision as to the use of equal marginal or equal absolute sacrifice as the appropriate basis of equity.

Even if these theoretical problems could be resolved, however, there would still remain the immense practical problems of acquiring enough information to estimate accurately the changes in utility stemming from different tax structures as seen by each individual. Since taxes are structured in terms of money units and ability to pay is a concept of justice based upon equal sacrifice in utility terms, it is necessary to find some means of utilizing an absolute cardinal scale of utility in addition. The difficulties in doing this in any but an arbitrary manner are prohibitive and the costs of acquiring unbiased information as to consumers' preferences, even if these difficulties were resolved, would delegate the ability to pay approach to the realm of theory as opposed to reality. It does not provide a feasible guide to actions in the positive model we have constructed.

Our positive approach to the process of taxation will thus have to abandon the appealing normative principles of the standard theory and replace them with a more realistic postulate. For want of a better name, we shall say that taxes are, in reality, determined in conjunction with an "ability-to-influence" principle. The exact nature of this principle will become clear in the remainder of this section. In general, it implies that taxes, like expenditures, are imposed through a process of political decision making, and that the results of this process stem from the patterns of influence that different groups are able to create. Those groups with the least political influence and power are most likely to feel the brunt of the tax burden, or at least of the total fiscal program.

THE POSITIVE APPROACH

Let us generally specify the environment in which tax burdens are determined within our model and then turn to an examination of the behavior of particular agents and groups of agents within this environment. In Part II we stressed the fact that it is the net effect of the tax and expenditure program which determines the distribution of real net benefits among individuals and groups. As a means of facilitating analysis, and even more because tax and expenditure decisions are made separately, we examined only the determination of the patterns of public demand. The tax structure was held constant. In this part we shall reverse this situation and regard the public purchase decisions as having already been made. The question with which we shall be concerned is the means by which the revenues necessary to finance this purchase program will be raised. There are any number of possible alternative programs of taxation. The government is given the responsibility of choosing among these.

Each of these alternatives involves different types of tax institutions and different burdens for different agents. The choice among these will have a strong impact on the distribution of real income in utility terms among the various segments of the model's society.

There are still four groups operating in our system, but only two of these are directly subject to taxation. Both consumers and producers are compelled to make certain payments to the government in return for a program of public expenditures. Once these payments have been determined by the government acting in its role as the public decision maker, consumers and producers are bound to pay them. They may affect their real burdens, however, by entering into the decision-making process. The other two groups, government and the bureaucracy, enter into the decision and administration aspects of taxation, but they are not subject to taxes in the performance of their functions.

Because of the practical difficulties in utilizing a large number of earmarked taxes, as the benefit principle would require, each taxpayer will be presented with a range of unearmarked taxes, each of which is used to finance a number of public transactions. The total tax bill may vary from individual to individual and from group to group, but each member of the two tax-paying categories is at least potentially subject to taxation.

This is not a particularly desirable situation from the point of view of these individuals, however, and our assumptions of rationality and self-interest will lead them to minimize the costs of taxation by engaging in influence production whenever it is profitable. With a given distribution of benefits from public purchasing programs, each taxpayer stands to realize a net gain if he can shift the costs of providing his share of the benefits onto other taxpayers. The greater the difference between the costs of public services (taxes) and the benefits of these services, the better off the individual is. In an uncertain world, with a government such as the one in our model, there is a potential for increasing this difference by producing influence which is brought to bear on the governmental decision-making process. As long as the costs of producing this influence are less than the gains to be made in the form of a reduced real tax burden, rational individuals and groups of individuals will use such influence. In other words, each agent is merely acting in such a manner as to alter the distribution of real income in his favor.

Government will be susceptible to this type of tax-reducing influence if it feels that by so doing it will realize a net improvement in its vote position. As in the case of purchasing, this susceptibility becomes increased substantially when uncertainty is present to any degree, and therefore in our model, influence will play an important role. To see this more clearly let us examine the behavior, first of taxpayers, and secondly of taxers, in some detail.

CHAPTER 8
CONSUMER BEHAVIOR UNDER TAXATION

> Anybody has a right to evade taxes if he can get away with it. No citizen
> has a moral obligation to assist in maintaining the government. If Con-
> gress insists on making stupid mistakes and passing foolish tax laws,
> millionaires should not be condemned if they take advantage of them.
>
> **J. Pierpont Morgan**

Consumers in the real world face a variety of tax institutions
which affect their behavior. Each of these is to some extent separated
from the purchases which it finances, though the degree of this separation will vary among different types of tax institutions. For example, the
isolation of educational expenditures from local property taxes is relatively small in most communities in the United States. Bond issues are
accepted for the specific purpose of providing educational services.
When we examine less localized expenditures, however, the degree of
separation increases substantially. The taxes paid to general funds which
support everything from foreign policy conferences, to national parks,
to highway subsidies, to fines of tuna fishermen paid to Ecuador, and
to White House parties are virtually indistinguishable from one another
as seen by the average consumer. For the most part taxes support a
rather generalized program of "public services" rather than specific
purchases, and hence we have assumed a range of unmarked taxes seen
by each consumer.

These taxes must be paid under the threat of legal penalty in
our system. They are coerced payments to cover the costs of all the
purchases of the single governing unit, and under complete certainty
and the appropriate institutional arrangements, they are necessary for
the attainment of a Paretian optimum. In an uncertain world their effects may not be unambiguously beneficial.

Taxes, examined in isolation, are definitely detrimental to the
welfare of consumers in fact. They reduce the disposable income of
consumers and hence reduce the purchases of utility-yielding goods
which can be made in the private sector. It is only in conjunction with
some program of expenditures that any real net gain is possible and

hence it is only this relationship which leads consumers to accept any positive taxation at all. A government or political party which proposed taxes in the absence of purchasing could not long endure within the framework of a democratic or republican form of governmental organization. Taxes do exist, however, and even though there is a degree of isolation involved, consumers regard them as some sort of general payments for the entire bundle of public services provided free of direct charges.

The introduction of these taxes will involve some significant adjustments in the behavior of consumers, both in the public and in the private sector. There will be market effects of taxation relevant to the choice of goods to be consumed and the work effect to be put forth. There will be political effects of taxation reflected in the voting choice of consumers and the perceived utility upon which they base this choice; these will also take the form of non-voting actions aimed at affecting the distribution of taxes by the government.

MARKET EFFECTS OF TAXATION

The effects that different taxes will have upon the problem of consumers' choice of goods and services have been discussed at some length in the normative literature. There are basically two types of market effects—those that pertain to the use of income and those that pertain to the choice of the total income to be earned. Taxes which are applied to specific goods only will introduce artificial alterations in the relative price ratios of goods, inducing a divergence between the actual marginal rates of substitution in production and the marginal rates of substitution in consumption. Widespread use of such taxes will create significant distortions in the allocation of resources within the private market as well as withdrawing resources to the public sector. In terms of the Lipsey–Lancaster second-best type of analysis, this implies that the best attainable situation in the presence of such taxes could involve departure from all the other Paretian conditions that would be satisfied in their absence.[1]

Taxes which are placed on all goods and services (in percent-

---

[1] Cf. R. G. Lipsey and K. Lancaster, "The General Theory of Second Best," *Review of Economic Studies*, Vol. XXIV, 1956–57, pp. 11–32. This analysis claims that social welfare may be improved in a situation where one optimal condition is unfulfilled, by allowing or causing other optimal conditions to become unfulfilled. The "best" solution is Pareto optimality in all markets. The "second-best" one may involve deviations in many markets if there is a deviation in one.

age terms) and taxes which are placed upon income will not have these distorting effects. They will serve merely to reduce the total real income available for purchasing goods and services, but they will not affect the relative prices at which these are traded. Such taxes may have an impact on the decision to work however, since they reduce the marginal benefit from an extra hour's labor, i.e., less income is available from each hour's work to be used on the purchase of goods and services since some of the wage must go to government in the form of taxes. This may lead individuals to work more hours in order to recoup their losses, or it may lead them to work fewer hours, substituting leisure for work. In theoretical terms, the ultimate effect of such taxation on work effort and productivity depends on the relative strengths of the income and substitution effects. In practical terms, institutional constraints limit the range of work-leisure options open to most individuals. With the exception of self-employed workers and some professionals the hours of labor are fixed according to the requirements of the employer, and may not be adjusted to fit individuals' differing marginal evaluations.

Taxes may also have effects upon the timing of consumption, i.e., whether to consume goods in the present rather than saving for future consumption. For example, taxes placed upon interest earned will reduce the gain from abstaining from present consumption and lead to decreases in the level of savings.

The number of potential tax institutions and the possibilities for using different tax bases are great. In each situation, the presence of taxes will have important market effects of the types briefly outlined above. Our major concern here is not with these market effects and the optimal choice between different types and bases of taxes. This question has already been examined in depth in the normative literature.[2] There are other effects of taxation that are of greater concern to us in this work—the effects it has on the political behavior of consumers. We will also see in later chapters in this part that the choice among all the possible tax institutions will not be made on the basis of normative considerations, but will arise from the political environment this behavior creates.

POLITICAL EFFECTS

The political behavior of consumers faced with the necessity of shifting resources from private to public use ranges from the choice of a means

[2] Cf., for example, Musgrave, op. cit., especially Chapters 11 and 12, for an analyses of the effects of different taxes on consumer choices.

of deciding how this shall be done to means of affecting the process of choice once it is established. As in the case of public expenditures, this first question is rationally answered only by utilizing representatives who make the actual decisions.

The Rationality of Representation

Each individual consumer is faced with a bundle of public expenditures which affects his total utility, and he is presented with a range of mandatory payments through which these programs are financed. These payments and the means by which they are collected will be decided through some process of collective choice. In some of the public finance literature it is customary to discuss the case where consumers vote directly on each tax-expenditure package.[3] In our model of an uncertain world, rationality will require that most decisions of this nature be made by representatives rather than direct participation.

The reasoning behind this statement closely parallels the reasoning behind the claimed necessity of representation in the choice of public purchasing programs. Consumers must not only bear the costs of taxation, they must also bear the costs involved in reaching collective decisions. These costs increase as the size of the deciding group increases and hence, past some point, it becomes irrational to expand the size of the group. It is cheaper to relinquish the right of participation in the decision to a representative who is charged with protecting the interests of his constituency. In exchange, consumers can participate in the choice of their representative through the election process.

Even if consumers were to participate directly in the tax distribution decision, the costs of doing so on an informed basis would far outweigh the gains. The extreme uncertainty as to the utility to be derived from public purchases which exhibit a degree of isolation can only be reduced by acquiring substantial amounts of information.[4] The gains which could be expected from the casting of a single ballot are quite small indeed if the deciding group becomes even moderately large. As a result it would be irrational to become sufficiently well informed to vote "intelligently" for each tax-expenditure package even

---

[3] Cf. James Buchanan, *Public Finance and the Democratic Process*, University of North Carolina Press, Chapel Hill, 1967, especially Part I.
[4] For a more complete discussion of this principle, see pages 54–55 in Part II.

in the absence of decision making costs. In their presence, the rationality of utilizing representation is made doubly strong, since it minimizes the costs of both acquiring information regarding each tax, and reaching collective decisions.

The Irrationality of Earmarked Taxes

We saw that the use of the normative principle of taxation according to benefit was made administratively unfeasible in a world of uncertainty. We can see now that it is also undesirable from the consumers' point of view to use it in such a situation. Consumers must pay not only for the purchases of the public sector but also for the administration of the fiscal program. The costs of setting and administering a large number of accurately earmarked taxes are substantially higher than those involved in collecting a single general tax, and the saving this implies may be enough to justify foregoing the allocative efficiency associated with earmarking.

Similarly, there are real costs involved in expressing preferences to representatives even when consumers do not vote directly on all tax programs. If governmental decisions are to reflect the preferences of the electorate, consumers will have to engage in non-voting influence since the selection of representatives does not provide a measure of these preferences. In most cases the potential gain from doing so will not justify these costs and hence consumers will permit most tax decisions to be made in ignorance of their preferences. There is, therefore, no reason to adopt a benefit type approach since it costs consumers more to administer, and it will still not provide any accurate means of actually distributing the burden according to benefit.

The rational behavior of consumers subject to taxation will lead them to accept tax bills which raise revenues for government expenditure in general. They will not take direct part in the determination of most taxes because the costs of so doing will outweigh the gain. They will be content to allow representatives to determine these tax bills, and they will often not even be aware of the existence of taxes let alone the manner in which they came into being. Only in a few cases which we shall discuss shortly will consumers be actively involved in tax decisions. In all other cases uncertainty and its effects isolate the distribution of taxes from consumers' utility functions.

Visibility of Timing. There are two general timing aspects of taxation. The first relates to the perpetuation of existing tax structures over time and is often summed up by the adage "an old tax is a good tax." In general, it implies that consumers will be less aware of a tax which has been in existence long enough for adjustments to have been made than of a tax which introduces new and unexpected distortions. Even if the actual burden is identical in the two forms of tax, the perceived burden fades with time until it is less than it was at the time of initiation.[7]

The second aspect of timing relates to the schedule of collection for a given tax. Presumably a tax collected regularly is more easily adjusted to, and becomes less visible, than a tax which is collected at irregular intervals, even if the total collection is the same in both cases. This aspect of visibility also applies to such fine timing considerations as the use of withholding in income tax collection. Withheld taxes are probably slightly less visible than they would be if individuals were given their gross pay and then required to pay the government directly from each pay check. (Note that withholding also makes income tax collection into a regular rather than irregular tax form and hence lowers visibility as discussed above.)

Visibility of Size. Since the imposition of a tax involves a loss of utility to the taxpayer, and since the greater the tax is, the greater will be this loss, we may expect a large tax to have a greater impact upon an individual than a small one. If the marginal utility of money is constant, the loss will be proportionately larger; if it is diminishing, the loss of utility will be more than proportionately greater with a large tax because the last dollar of taxation will "hurt" more than the first one. This implies that a series of small taxes may be less visible than a single large tax, particularly over time if small losses are more easily forgotten than larger ones.

Each tax institution has a certain degree of visibility which is a function of these three characteristics. A low visibility tax will be perceived as having a lower burden than a highly visible tax of the same absolute amount. Since voters' behavior in elections depends upon the perceived utility of public tax and expenditure programs, the visibility of different tax institutions will be of great importance in determining the structure of taxes used to finance government programs. For any

---

[7] For a discussion of this point, see Buchanan, *op. cit.*, Chapter 5.

given bundle of expenditures, the tax program which presents the least visible taxes will be the vote maximizing one.

The Role of Information. The relationship between perceived and actual tax burdens depends not only on the purely structural characteristics which we have termed "visibility" but also on the information any given consumer has as to the real nature of his liability. Given a positive cost of acquiring information, we have concluded that it is irrational to attempt to estimate one's actual burden under low visibility taxes since the costs of doing so will exceed the gain. Even if one were completely aware of the total tax burden to which he was subject, the chances that his single vote for a representative, who will decide a vast number of tax-expenditure issues, could effectively improve his situation are minute. When this awareness is quite costly to acquire, uninformed responses to taxation become rational. It will not be beneficial to invest resources in an effort to determine actual tax burdens.

However, complete uncertainty is undoubtedly not an optimal situation from the consumer's point of view and certain amounts of information available at no direct cost may be assimilated by consumers. This opens the way for the influence of consumer behavior by subsidizing the acquisition of information which selectively affects the perception of tax burdens. Since governments are elected on the basis of consumers' expected utility over the future, and since a lower perceived tax burden increases this expected utility a political party should attempt to reduce the level of perceived burdens as long as the expected gain in votes exceeds the costs of influence. Voters should be susceptible to this influence since it reduces uncertainty, though they may discount the subsidized information.

VOTER INFLUENCE OF TAX BURDENS

Each taxpayer has some perceived value for a tax burden, and he has an awareness that public action is imposing costs on him at least equal to this amount. With a given program of expenditures it is in the interest of each individual taxpayer to have this burden reduced by shifting some of the costs of public programs onto other taxpayers. Such a shift would represent an unambiguous increase in his utility since it would not alter the stream of benefits he derives from collective action and it would leave him with a higher income to be spent in the private market. There are a number of ways in which individuals and groups may try to induce the government to engage in such shifts of tax burden. These all involve real and often substantial costs, however, and they will only be utilized when the incentive in the form of expected reductions in tax burdens justifies it.

Voting

The first and most common method of attempting to shift tax burdens is the use of the ballot. In reality, the difficulties of affecting particular tax policies by voting for representatives are many and they have been discussed at length above. They render the expected gain from this particular method of influence quite small. Nevertheless, it is commonly used because it is by far the least expensive means of influence in terms of real resources required. Except in the most general sense, it is highly ineffective and individuals with a strong incentive will utilize other means of influence instead. The use of the vote may result in a few specific types of tax policy however. Because of the extremely high proportion of low-income voters relative to high-income ones, that party which proposes progressivity in the nominal tax rates should command a majority, other things equal. The ballot can be used by low-income voters as a group in an attempt to shift their tax burden to the rich.

Similarly, since only consumers vote directly in our model, we would also expect to see the vote used to shift taxes from consumers in general to producers in general. Any party which proposed large scale increases in the direct taxation of consumers in order to relieve producers would find a serious deterioration in its vote position. These general characteristics will not always exhaust the possibilities for improvement in the positions of agents through influence. Those who feel that they can realize a net increase in real income by producing influence will thus turn to methods other than direct voting.

Non-Voting Influence

Government in our model is a vote maximizer. It realizes that voters make their decisions on the basis of perceived utility, but it is not certain as to the perceptions or the preference functions of individuals. As a result it suffers from uncertainty as to which actions will really improve its vote position, and it is susceptible to influence in the form of subsidized information as to the nature and intensity of voter preferences. If one group of consumers sees a sufficient benefit from the enactment of a particular tax policy, it may be willing to incur the costs implied by this subsidization. It involves much higher costs than voting per se, but the probability of successfully influencing public decisions is substantially increased. This is particularly true when there is no counterbalancing program of influence production being undertaken by opposing groups or individuals.

The information provided to governments may also stress the secondary effects of government tax policy and in turn the impact on votes of these considerations. For example, some groups of consumers may claim that a tax on municipal bonds would lead them to seek other forms of financial investment and that a serious crisis in terms of local finance would result. This subsidized information may state or merely imply that such a situation would not be favorable to the government's goal of retaining office. In either case, non-voting influence may take the form of subsidizing government's acquisition of the information upon which it will base its tax decision.

A modification of this type of influence is found when consumers provide other voters, who are also uncertain as to the size of their actual tax burden, with selective information as to the nature of this liability. Arguments in the public arena for and against proposed policies often stress the fact that they will have adverse effects upon voters' taxes. Indeed, there are many cases where opposing sides have both claimed that their adversaries' position implied an increase in taxes, leading undoubtedly to a certain amount of confusion on the part of voters.

Some groups of voters may influence others by providing accurate data as to the nature of tax liabilities. Others may be more willing to modify the facts at their disposal in their attempts at influence.

Consumer influence of governmental tax decisions need not center directly around the use of information. As we have seen in Parts I and II of this work, political parties use substantial amounts of resources to subsidize consumers' acquisition of information to be used in making voting decisions. By subsidizing selective information they may be able to alter voters' perceived utility streams from governmental action and hence alter their voting decision. We also noted that it is necessary for governments or parties to acquire these resources from other agents in the system—partly through taxation and partly through trade. Election requires control over resources, control which will not be granted in a society of self-interested individuals without some benefit offered in return. Trades of this sort need not be explicit. It is enough that parties are aware of policies which are beneficial to potential contributors and adopt them. The contributors, seeing a potential gain from the election of a party espousing this position, may provide resources with which they hope to assure the gain.

The offer of resources may be quite explicit, however, unless the fear of scandal scares either party away from the trade. In terms of tax policies, the trade of resources for favorable positions introduces an unusual consideration. A party may adopt a tax policy which by itself results in a net loss of votes if, in the party's estimation, the resources forthcoming from contributors will be great enough to influence voters' decisions to the extent that there will be an overall improvement in its vote position.

To be sure, there are very substantial costs to consumers who engage in influence of this variety, but for those individuals and groups for whom the potential gain is greater yet, our recurrent theme of rationality requires them to incur these costs. Indeed, there is empirical evidence that individuals and groups which benefit from the tax concessions of oil depletion allowances provide rather substantial financial support to those candidates for office who appear to be strongly in favor of such policies.

There are obviously a number of forms which consumer attempts to influence governmental decisions on tax distribution may take. These generally utilize resources in trades or in the subsidization of information acquisition. All involve costs, but in some cases these costs will be justified. We will consider these cases in more detail shortly, but first let us turn to an examination of the types of shifts in tax burden which may result from the use of these types of influence.

POSSIBLE SHIFTS IN CONSUMER TAX BURDENS

We have postulated that only producers and consumers pay taxes in our system and hence all shifts of tax burdens will have to take place either within or between these two sectors. The first and most obvious type of shift for consumers to attempt is to try to reduce their burdens by increasing the taxes paid by producers. Governments will generally facilitate this desire for a shift up to some point. Producers as such do not vote, and hence the obvious shifting of visible tax from the consumer sector onto the producer sector will result in an increase in perceived utility streams. This cannot be done to too great an extent lest the resources forthcoming from producers be given to competing parties. It is also important to note that much of the actual burden of the new producer taxes may be borne by consumers in the form of higher prices paid for goods and services. However, since this new burden is far less visible than the old one, the perceived tax burden of consumers will be lower even if the actual burden is unchanged.

The gain to any one consumer from causing such a shift in tax liabilities will generally not be sufficient to justify substantial expenditures for influence. Such shifts will generally arise from pressures placed by consumers as a group in the electoral process and will become fact when a party attempts to realize the potential gain in votes that the shift implies. Producers, either individually or collectively, may produce influence aimed at countering this tendency but they will probably not be able to eliminate it entirely.

Given the wide variety of potential tax institutions, there will exist a great number of possible shifts in tax burden from one subset of consumers to another. For example, taxes may be levied on the basis of different income levels, on either property or non-property income, on urban or suburban voters, on the sales of necessities or luxuries, etc. The use of any of these institutions implies a gain for some individual taxpayers at the expense of others.

In the case of income taxes we have seen that there will be a tendency toward nominal progressivity in tax rates as the large number of lower-income voters uses its voting power to influence its tax burden. Nominal taxes will be determined by a progressive structure. This raises the incentive for upper-income individuals to engage in influence with regard to government decisions in order to reduce the effects of progressivity.

In fact, under either a progressive or proportional nominal tax structure, high-income individuals face a higher expected gain from shifting tax burdens in an absolute sense than do low-income individuals. Their nominal tax bill is higher than that of low-income individuals; its elimination represents a greater absolute gain.

If we assume that the costs of influencing tax decisions are independent of one's income position, we would expect to see far more influence produced by upper-income individuals and groups. As a result we would also expect to see rather severe reductions in effective tax rates for upper-income individuals to the extent that this influence is successful. It will not be countered to any great degree by the actions of lower income individuals since their potential gain will not often justify the costs.[8]

If the costs of producing influence are inversely related to the level of one's income, as some have suggested, then this tendency for greater production on the part of upper-income groups will be stronger still.[9] This could be because of the closer social ties between wealthy individuals and members of government which grant easy access to decision makers which is unavailable to those on the other end of the income distribution.

Since there are fewer high- than low-income individuals, these tendencies toward effective tax reduction for the former may be reinforced because of the relatively low costs of organization. It is easier to organize a small group for effective action than a large one, and a group where each individual stands to realize a significant absolute gain makes organization easier yet.[10]

The determination of the "optimal" tax institutions from the point of view of the influencing individual and group depends upon their asset portfolios and income positions. It is likely that there are a number of potential tax policies which will effectively shift the real burden of taxation from influencers to non-influencers. This carries a number of implications regarding the nature of the overall tax program which will be followed by a vote maximizing government. We will examine this in some detail shortly, but we generally predict that it will consist of a highly progressive nominal tax structure which is quite visible to the voting public. In practice, however, the actual tax burden will be distributed far less progressively in response to the influence we can expect to be forthcoming from upper income groups. The necessary shortage of revenues will then be eliminated by utilizing regressive, but highly invisible taxes which do not have significant effects on

[8] A detailed discussion of the groups expected to engage in influence production takes place in Part IV, Non-Voting Influence.
[9] Cf., for example, C. Wright Mills, *The Power Elite*, Oxford University Press, London, 1956, and also, cf. Anthony Downs, *op. cit.*, especially his discussion of the "costs of communication."
[10] In this regard, see Mancur Olson, Jr., *The Logic of Collective Action*, Schocken Books, New York, 1965; see also the discussion of his work in Part IV of this book.

the perceived tax burdens of lower income individuals. There may be a certain amount of subsidized political information provided by government and parties which stresses "appropriate" characteristics of this tax system.

CONCLUSIONS

The programs carried out by the collective body require some means of financing. This implies, in the framework of our model, that some purchasing power will be withdrawn from the private sector in the form of taxation. Consumers in this system are primary subjects of this taxation and its presence has significant effects upon their behavior in both the market environment and the political arena. We have been able to reach a number of conclusions about this behavior:

1. Taxes, even though they affect all consumers, will not be determined by consumers acting directly in the decision making process. In order to minimize the costs of collection, decision making, and information, tax decisions, like public purchasing decisions, will be made by elected representatives.
2. Taxes, examined in isolation, reduce consumers utility from the market in two ways—they will lower the real disposable income of consumers and they will introduce distortions into relative price ratios. These are the "market effects" of taxation. Taxes in conjunction with public spending may or may not increase consumers utility from the market.
3. Consumers' views of the utility outcome of government action determine their political responses to taxation. Their votes will depend upon the perceived value of their tax burdens relative to the perceived value of utility derived from government action. The perceived value of this burden will depend upon the visibility of tax institutions and the price of information relevant to the nature of actual tax burdens.
4. Given a stream of benefits from collective action, it is in the interest of any consumer or group of consumers to shift the costs of such action onto other taxpayers. Whenever the costs of influencing governmental tax decisions are less than the gains to be made from such shifts, consumers will attempt to cause them.
5. Voter influence of government decisions regarding tax burdens may take a number of forms. These range from relatively inexpen-

sive methods such as voting to far more expensive means of non-voting influence such as campaign contributions. Lower income voters as a whole will generally use less expensive means such as voting; upper income consumers will be more likely, and have a greater incentive, to utilize non-voting means of direct influence.

6. As a result of these conclusions there are a number of predictions we could make regarding the nature of the tax structure to be expected. Consumers as a whole would shift some of their burden onto producers through the process of voting. Producers may shift some back in the form of higher prices but there will be some net shift. The nominal structure of rates will be progressive because of the greater number of lower income voters. The actual impact of the rates will be less progressive because of consciously instigated shifts in burden in response to influence from upper income groups. The increased regressivity of effective tax burdens will be disguised by using low visibility, regressive tax institutions.

7. Consumers, in their responses to taxation, are subject once again to uncertainty, and as a result to influence of their actions. In turn, they may take advantage of the uncertainty surrounding other agents to attempt to improve their relative and absolute positions.

CHAPTER 9
PRODUCER
BEHAVIOR
UNDER TAXATION

There is really no way of forcing a successful profit-making corporation to pay taxes other than by levying on its capital, thereby reducing it at least as fast as retained earnings build it up.

Ferdinand Lundberg

The burden of supplying revenues to finance public purchases is nominally shared in our system by both consumers and producers. Different types of tax institutions will obviously affect the two groups differently, but each producer and each consumer will face some real tax burden. Similarly we have postulated that each producer and each consumer could conceivably derive a stream of benefits from the actions of government in the public sector. Nevertheless, the behavior of the two groups in the face of taxation is not identical and hence it will be valuable to examine the behavior we would expect within the producing sector of our economy.

As with consumers, there are two basic types of behavioral effects caused in producers' actions by the introduction of taxation—"market" effects and "political" effects. The former category consists of adjustments in the market behavior of firms as their costs are altered by the imposition of taxes. These effects are widely discussed and are standard fare for textbooks in public finance theory. The latter category consists of those actions firms take to try to alter the tax burden they face. These actions will be aimed at influencing the decisions on tax policy which are made in the public sector. These effects are not covered as frequently, yet they represent the major modifications in behavior once we move from normative to positive models.

MARKET EFFECTS OF TAXATION

There are a variety of tax institutions designed to acquire revenues from the producing sector. These range from corporate income taxes to property taxes to taxes on inputs to taxes on outputs to licensing fees. Each type of institution will have important effects, though the nature of these effects differs from institution to institution. It is interesting to note that most taxes on producers involve highly visible tax structures, however. Most of them are collected as a separate item isolated from direct market action. Moreover, the accounting practices required by business firms carefully specify the expenditures that are to meet tax liabilities in most cases except when they result from higher prices of taxed inputs. Therefore, even though it is an obvious simplification, we shall postulate that producers, unlike consumers, make their market (and political) decisions on the basis of their actual tax burdens. By this we mean that the perceived tax liability from any action a firm decides to take coincides with the actual burden; taxes on producers are highly visible to producers.

The first type of market adjustment producers may make to taxation involves changes in their price and output decisions. Musgrave notes that taxes on units of output will result in reductions in output and increases in price no matter what the form of the market structure. The degree of price change is affected by this structure, however, with monopolists raising price by only half of the increase to be expected under perfect competition. Similarly, ad valorem taxes will result in reductions in output and increases in the prices a firm will charge as well.[1]

Taxes on firms may also have market effects in terms of alterations in the investment decisions which the firms make. These effects will differ depending upon the degree of loss offset included in the liability of the producer. Taxation may affect either the composition of the investment portfolio or the size of the portfolio in the case of financial as opposed to real investments. The methods under which firms may treat depreciation of capital equipment in the tax law will also affect the timing and the choice of investment decisions, as will the treatment of interest costs.[2]

Finally, the effects that taxation has upon investment decisions

---

[1] For a complete discussion of this phenomenon, see Musgrave, *op. cit.*, Chapter 13. It is important to note that not all analysts agree with the usual conclusion that corporate taxes are paid by corporations. Those who reject the concept of competition and claim instead that prices and even wants are largely administered insist that taxes are always and completely passed on to consumers in the form of higher prices. See, for example, Ferdinand Lundberg, *The Rich and the Super Rich*, Lyle Stuart, Inc., New York, 1968, especially pp. 353–357.

[2] Cf. Musgrave, *op. cit.*

will alter the rate and the structure of capital accumulation and through this the growth of the economy as a whole and its orientation toward different types of outputs.

In very brief fashion this is a review of the expected types of alterations in market behavior stemming from taxation. Taxes on producers are essentially additions to costs, and as all price theorists are aware, the costs faced by a producer are key determinants in his behavior. The literature abounds with analyses of these effects and hence we shall be content with the cursorily presented picture of the previous paragraphs. More important from our point of view is an examination of the effects which the presence of a real or potential tax burden will have on the political behavior of producers.

POLITICAL EFFECTS OF TAXATION

We shall continue to assume a fixed program of governmental expenditures as in the case of consumers. Firms will receive a certain stream of benefits from these expenditures which is not affected by the tax structure which raises the necessary revenues. However, any reduction in the real burden of a firm represents a net increase in its profits, and since we have specified profit maximization as the goal of all firms, any reduction is desirable from their point of view. For this reason we would expect to see a firm shifting its tax burden onto other taxpaying units whenever the *ex ante* estimation of the gain in terms of reduced taxes is greater than the *ex ante* estimation of the costs of causing change.

Taxes are still imposed through the political process by elected representatives of consumers. However, the costs of information and the presence of uncertainty combine to isolate effectively these representatives from the real preferences of the electorate. As a result there arises an opportunity for producers to affect their tax liability by using resources to create political influence. There are a number of ways in which this influence can be exerted.

Methods of Influence

Tax burdens are determined in conjunction with a desire to maximize votes. In our system producers as such do not vote for representatives, so direct voting is not a viable means of influencing their tax burdens.

This does not imply that they cannot use other methods of exerting influence. In fact, our assumption of rationality will sometimes require them to produce influence.

Even though producers cannot vote, they may be able to affect the decisions of those who do vote, and through them they may alter the decisions of those in power. Because of the high level of uncertainty surrounding consumers in their determination of the expected value of utility streams, they will be subject to subsidized information as a form of influencing their estimates and hence their voting decisions. Producers may take advantage of this situation and attempt to lead consumers to favor strongly tax policies which are beneficial to the producers.

For example, a firm could engage in a public relations campaign which stresses the probable increase in prices consumers would have to pay as a result of increased taxes on producers. It could at the same time raise the relative price of information relating to the decrease to be expected in consumers' direct taxes. Or producers in a particular industry could campaign openly for tax and tariff policies that protect their position in the market by stressing the dangers of "cheap" foreign labor and the patriotism of buying at home. To the extent that firms are able to alter successfully consumers' expected utility streams, and to the extent they are able to make the government aware of these alterations, they will be able to influence tax policy.

A second method of influencing tax policy is based on the fact that government is also uncertain as to the exact nature of consumers' preferences. Firms may openly lobby in the seat of government for particular policies and may provide the results of "unbiased research" to the members of government at a subsidized rate. Undoubtedly they will be less anxious to provide information they have which is detrimental to their ends. As with consumers, this may stress either direct effects of policies on votes, or it may provide information on secondary effects which involve utility affecting phenomena.

A third and final form of possible influence involves only indirect manipulation of voters' expected utility and involves primarily shifts in the control over resources. The producing sector controls vast quantities of real resources which could be used by parties seeking office to finance the subsidization of political information to the electorate. Other things equal, the party providing the most selective information will be elected. As a result firms may agree, implicitly or explicitly, to provide parties, including the incumbent one, with campaign resources.

In exchange for the use of these resources, firms may expect the adoption of tax policies favorable to their goal of profit maximization. This exchange need not take the form of vulgar back room deals to be effective. All that is necessary is that the party involved know that a firm is benefited by certain policies and that the firm is an active (or behind the scenes) supporter of the party. It should then reach the conclusion on its own that opposition to these policies implies a termination of the support.

There are real costs involved in all of these forms of influence, but as always, to the extent that a real net gain can be expected from utilizing them, rational firms will do so. Not all firms will engage in direct influence and not all of those that do will use the same techniques for the same purpose. We can make certain predictions about the strategies followed by different types of firms in different market situations, but we shall defer this discussion for a few pages until we outline a number of possible shifts in tax burdens.

Possible Shifts in Burden

Producers faced with a potential tax burden may engage in shifting activities of two general types. They may attempt to shift the burden of taxation onto other agents within the producing sector or they may try to shift it onto other types of taxpayers, i.e., consumers. In both situations the shift may be accomplished within the market, or it may result from the political activity of firms.

Producer to Producer Shifts.   There are two types of benefit possible for a producer who can shift his tax burdens onto other producers. The first of these is quite obvious—by increasing another's tax liability he may be reducing his own. The second form of benefit was not present in the case of consumers, and is probably of greater importance than the first. This benefit has to do with tax policies and shifts which improve the position of the firm in the market. Taxes placed upon competitors may raise their costs enough to significantly affect their share of the market favorably. Specific excise taxes placed upon goods for which there are substitutes will be desirable from the point of view of the producers of those substitutes. Tariffs placed upon the importation of

A rational producer considering an attempted shift of tax burdens onto consumers will have to take into account two secondary effects of such action. First, he would have to consider the alterations in consumers' real disposable income after the tax shift and the effects of these on the demand for the commodities he produces. If all prices charged by the producing sector fall sufficiently as a result of the reduction in their direct taxes, there may be no significant effects on real demand. In this case, however, the benefit to be derived from tax shifting is questionable since it implies merely trading a market induced shift for a politically induced shift. As we have stated, it seems apparent that the costs of causing such a trade for a producer would seem quite high. If all prices do not drop significantly, then the real demand faced by the firm may actually drop. Hence a producer must consider the expected effects of the induced shift on the real incomes of consumers, and on the relative price shifts in goods.

Secondly, the producer should consider the relative nature of the income elasticity of the goods he produces. In the likely event that politically induced shifts in taxation involve real decreases in the disposable incomes of at least a class of consumers, the effects on the demands for all products will not be the same. We could expect to see the demand faced by producers of luxury items more severely affected than that faced by producers of necessities.

If, after due consideration of these possibilities, a firm feels that it will benefit from a politically induced shift of taxes onto the consuming sector, it will utilize one of the methods of non-voting influence discussed above. If a market shift is possible, it is preferable because of the lower costs involved, but if it is not possible, and if the expected gain justifies the costs, political means will be used.

PREDICTED PATTERNS OF PRODUCER RESPONSE TO TAXATION

Firms in the producing sector will find direct taxation placed upon them a hindrance in their pursuit of profits, either because it directly reduces them or because it reduces the firms' competitive positions in their markets. Firms will respond to taxation by attempting to escape its "burden" whenever it is feasible to do so, given the costs of such escape. The actual strategy followed by any particular firm is difficult to predict in the absence of extensive data. However, there are a few general predictions we can make regarding the expected response of the producing sector to taxation.

First, much of the tax burden nominally placed upon producers will, in actuality, be shifted onto consumers. This will most often take place through increases in the prices of goods which we termed "market" responses to taxes. The degree to which shifting of this variety can be carried out depends upon the structure of the market and the elasticity of consumer demand. It is particularly appealing as a method of shifting because of its low visibility and relatively low costs of administration. On occasion, but far less often than market shifts, political shifts in taxes from producers to consumers will be attempted. The higher direct costs of engaging in influence necessary to do this and the higher visibility of such action makes it less appealing to both producers and the government.

Political action will be used in attempts to alter taxes by producers, but we would expect it to be used most often in the protection of the competitive position of a firm. The taxes which are involved in actions such as these have effects which cannot be easily produced by purely market phenomena; they require extra market action in the form of legal decisions. The protection of domestic industries by tariffs is not directly comparable with any form of pure market activity. In these cases the higher costs and higher visibility of direct political action may be justifiable from the point of view of the firm.

We would not expect to see all firms engaged in equal amounts of political action aimed at influencing their tax burdens however. There is reason to believe that the amount of political activity may be directly correlated with the size of the producing unit. The protection of an industry will provide larger gains per firm if there are fewer firms than if there are many. Firms with a large share of the market stand to gain more than firms with only a marginal interest in the total production. If the costs of creating influence are independent of size, we would nevertheless tend to see only larger firms producing it.

If, as is more likely, there are certain economies of scale in the production of influence, e.g., the president of General Motors has easier access to high members of government than the owner of the local gas station, this situation is reinforced. The net benefit from political influence of tax policies will be greater for larger firms. Going one step further, and anticipating the discussion of Olson's work in the next Part we might also note that policies which affect a large number of firms are "collective" goods. It may not be rational for many small firms to incur the costs of influence while it may be rational for one large firm to do so. Moreover, the costs of organizing large numbers of small firms to take advantage of the collective nature of the policy may easily become prohibitively expensive.

We could predict then that firms in competitive industries would engage in very little political activity with regard to the nature of their individual taxes while oligopolistic firms would be far more inclined to do so. Presumably government tax policies would reflect this and tend to offer certain benefits to large firms in oligopolistic industries as a result of political pressure of one type or another.

CONCLUSIONS

Taxation interferes with the goal of the producing sector—the maximization of profits. Producers react to this interference in a manner consistent with our assumptions of rationality and self-interest. They will attempt to influence the distribution of the tax burden and the choice of tax institutions both in their market and in their political actions. The decision to enter the tax problem and the choice of the appropriate means of influence depend upon the nature of the costs and benefits of such action. Producers may use tax policy to protect their position in their markets or they may attempt to shift the tax burdens they face onto other taxpayers. In any case, producers are not passive respondents to tax policy. In their rational pursuit of their self-interest they will enter the problem of determining tax policies as very active participants. Some will participate more than others and the outcome of the governmental decision-making process will reflect this.

CHAPTER 10
GOVERNMENTAL DETERMINATION OF TAX POLICIES

·... [Tax] actions reflect the pressures on the Congressmen. The influence of the groups arrayed against a significant redistribution of the tax burden is enormous, and there is no effect lobby for the poor and near poor.

Joseph Pechman

... it would be strange if taxation by interest groups should not result in taxation according to interest.

Knut Wicksell

The extensive costs involved in reaching decisions in large groups, of administering taxes, and of acquiring information in the face of gross uncertainty will lead to the presence of certain obvious characteristics of the tax program in our model. First, the responsibility for decision making in the determination of tax burdens will be delegated to a relatively small group of representatives whose overall actions are subject to periodic approval by the electorate. This group is, of course, the government. Secondly, large taxes which are used to finance a number of purchases in the public sector will be used in the place of a detailed schedule of earmarked taxes. Thirdly, it should be apparent by now that the voting for representatives does not offer any effective means of discovering voter preferences. Governmental decisions are made in ignorance of consumer preferences in the absence of some form of non-voting influence. Taxpayers, in both the producing and consuming sectors, who have particularly strong interests in certain tax measures, will attempt to utilize political influence to insure that these interests enter the decision-making process. Much of the influence of this type, which was discussed in the previous two sections, was assumed to be effective. We shall now see why.

GOVERNMENTAL SUSCEPTIBILITY

As before, those in office desire to remain in office, and those outside desire to attain it. In a democratic system such as the one we have postulated the only means of acquiring control of government is to receive a majority of the votes cast in elections. Following Downs, we have therefore claimed that political parties formulate policies in order to get elected rather than seek office in order to establish some "best" set of policies. Under this type of motivation for government, tax policies will adhere to "benefit" or "ability-to-pay" criteria only when such criteria maximize expected votes. There is no a priori reason to assume that they would do so. The determination of tax burdens will depend upon the pressures brought to bear successfully on the government.

Governments, like all other agents in our system, are uncertain as to much important information relevant to its decisions. First, since voting is not an effective means of acquiring information as to consumers' preferences with respect to particular programs, governments are not really aware of the actual effects of their tax and expenditure programs. The actual value of the burden of a tax on an individual is less easy to determine ex ante (or even ex post) than the nominal burden. Hence governments are uncertain as to both voter preferences and the effects of their actions upon the variables included in those preference functions.

We have also discussed the possibility of divergences between actual and perceived tax burdens as viewed by consumers. Here again the level of uncertainty involved in governmental decisions is increased. Even if government knew exactly how a program would affect the variables in the system and how these would influence consumer behavior if known, it would still be uncertain as to the awareness of consumers with regard to these effects. As a result government will, by necessity, make most of its decisions on the basis of highly imperfect information. Complete uncertainty is undoubtedly undesirable since it decreases the chances of election and so we would expect government to engage in the acquisition of at least limited amounts of information. Given the costs of such action government will be susceptible to the subsidization of this process as well as to the implicit or explicit offer of real resources in trade for favorable tax policies. The influence it feels may be created through any one of a number of approaches, but whenever the influence alters government's *perception* of its abilities to gain votes, it will alter its behavior. The influence need not actually alter the votes of consumers —it only need alter government's perception of such votes and preferences.

TYPES OF INFLUENCE

Voting

Since governments are primarily concerned with votes, those agents which vote can use this to influence policy decisions. The degree of influence any one vote can have over any one policy is extremely small but nevertheless positive. This influence can be increased if the government is provided with subsidized information stressing the dependence of the vote on one particular action. This is along the lines of Downs' discussions of the most intensive desires of voters. For example, a voter claiming that he will support whichever party promises to reduce property taxes regardless of other policies will increase the influence his vote has over that one issue, *provided* the government is made aware of the intensity of this desire. As Downs notes, a rational government will often be able to improve its vote position by catering to the most intense desires of minorities. This obviously requires some action in addition to pure voting however.

Information on Preferences

Governments realize that voters cast their ballots on the basis of their utility functions. In order to propose policies which will attract votes, government should therefore have some knowledge of consumer preference functions. It will be glad to acquire information relating to these, particularly when it is offered at a subsidized price. Direct lobbying, letter writing campaigns, mass demonstrations and public opinion polls (the results of which tend to be partially a function of who commissions the poll) are all means of providing subsidized but selective information of this nature. Government will accept this information, though it may apply a discount factor to it, and will make its decisions on the basis of it. To the extent that the information is selectively biased, the decisions of government will reflect this.

Information of the Results of Programs

Governments are also unaware of all of the ramifications of the programs which they propose. The selective pricing of information as to the effects of these programs which government will view as favorable to its vote position may alter the mix of programs accepted. For example, studies showing the beneficial effects of tax credits for investment in terms of increased employment are made known to the government at low cost. Information on results of a tax program which will be detrimental to vote maximization will be less freely offered by agents who would benefit from the enactment of the tax measure.

Resources for Governmental Use

We outlined above the need for government to use real resources in the influence of consumers' utility functions if it is to retain office. It can acquire some of these resources through the process of taxation itself, but a majority of them must come from members of the private sector in the form of trades. They are presented to government in response to the governmental enactment of policies which are favorable to their owners. In this case government will be susceptible to such influence even if the proposed action itself will not directly increase votes. All that is necessary is that the gain in votes expected from the use of these resources plus the gain in votes from enactment *together* exceed the loss in votes that enactment implies. Governmental influence of consumer behavior using these resources may either be aimed at raising voters' estimation of the utility to be derived from public expenditures or it may lower their perceived tax burden. The resources need not be applied directly to issues relating to the tax measure which generated them.

Government will therefore be susceptible to influence through resource transfers whenever its *ex ante* estimation of the situation leads to an expected increase in votes. This estimation is more likely to favor successful influence the lower is the degree of visibility of the increase in tax burdens on other agents and the greater is government's perception of its ability to influence consumers' expected utility. Both of these factors, in turn, depend on the degree of uncertainty on the part of voters faced with positive information costs. The greater the level of voter uncertainty, the more susceptible government will be to resource transfer influence. The greater the level of government uncertainty, the more it will be susceptible to the other three types of influence discussed.

Given that all agents in our system suffer from a rather high degree of uncertainty, particularly with regard to activities in the public realm, we would expect to see government exhibiting susceptibility to all types of influence in significant amounts.

OPTIMAL TAX STRATEGY FOR GOVERNMENT

There are certain aspects of the tax structure arising out of the governmental decision process which we can predict. The characteristics of the total tax program will reflect government's vote maximization desires and the pattern of influence exerted on the decision by interested taxpayers.

First, government will visibly shift a large segment of the tax burden onto the producing sector since producers as such do not vote. It will also provide consumers with subsidized information as to the extent of the nominal burden placed upon producers. The effective burden will be substantially less, however, since producers will shift much of this burden back onto consumers through market as opposed to political action. Producers will be taxed, but consumers will bear much of the burden in the form of higher prices, a method of shifting which involves extremely low visibility.

Secondly, the rate structure and forms of taxes imposed upon the producing sector will reflect a certain amount of political pressure. We would expect the tax program to strengthen the relative market positions of those firms who engage in the production of political influence. We have seen, however, that firms in oligopolistic industries will be more likely to engage in such activity than firms in highly competitive ones. There will thus appear to be a certain amount of circularity in the process. Oligopolistic firms will be able to benefit from political activity aimed at the tax decision in the form of a protected market share. Firms in protected markets in turn constitute oligopolies.

Third, taxes will be placed directly upon consumers in visible form. However, a vote maximizing government aware of the excess of low-income voters over upper-income ones will openly propose highly progressive nominal tax rates. Government should also subsidize low-income voters' acquisition of information as to the degree of the nominal progressivity. However, in order to increase the likelihood of receiving votes, it should allow every voter a reduction of one form or another. It should make each voter's own reductions obvious to him, but be less insistent that he be made aware of other voters' tax breaks.

The effective rates of taxation should be lower than the nominal rates, across the board. The reduction should be obvious only with regard to one's own tax burden.

Fourth, the reduction in effective rates will be relatively greater for those at the top of the income distribution than for those at the bottom. As shown above, the absolute gain from a reduction in taxes is greater for high-income individuals under progressivity, and the costs of causing such a change are lower because of lower costs of communication and organization. This reduction will be the result of political activity, either in the form of information subsidization, or more likely in the form of resource transfers. Lower income individuals often will not be able to realize a net gain from such political activity.

Finally, it will be necessary to increase the real tax yield from other types of taxes to make up for the reduction in real revenues from income taxation. This must be done, of course, with an eye towards the reactions of consumers as reflected in their voting decisions. Therefore, the increase in regressivity should result from the introduction of highly invisible taxes, including even the use of corporate taxes which are passed on to consumers in the form of higher prices. If this is done successfully, consumers perceived tax burdens will be far lower than their actual ones, particularly on the lower end of the income scale. The effect on votes of such action may also be minimized if consumers look at the value of their tax burden relative to other's. If a consumer's perceived tax burden is relatively low compared to the taxes he *perceives* others paying, he may regard his share as just. To the extent that the government can utilize a structure which appears progressive in the visible institutions, it may be able to lower the estimates that low-income voters have of their own burdens and raise their estimates of the burden on high-income voters.

Government may also utilize certain forms of non-tax financing for public programs if it feels that these institutions will improve its overall vote position. A strategy such as the one we have outlined here, including perhaps a certain amount of non-tax financing, will provide government with a maximum of direct votes and a substantial supply of resources with which to influence further votes.

NON-TAX FINANCING

There are, in addition to the various tax institutions, certain methods of non-tax financing that are available to governments in their determination of fiscal programs. The two most obvious forms of such financing are the use of debt finance and of an "inflation tax." The actual impact of utilizing these methods is subject to some debate in the literature, and it is not our purpose here to arbitrate this debate. We merely wish to recognize explicitly their existence and to point out that they can be analyzed within the framework we have been applying to methods of tax financing.

For example, it is commonly noted that debt financing can be a useful tool in the government's attempts at fostering overall stability and full employment in the economy. We have no quarrel with this; but we wish to introduce the notion that the use of debt for this purpose will have different effects upon the vote position of a government than will other policies leading to the same ends of stabilization and full employment. A vote maximizing government will take account of these differences in its choice of policies and instruments.

Indeed, it may be tempting to point to all of the other implications and uses of various financing programs, such as influencing monetary conditions, stimulating investment, etc., and to claim that these determine the choice of tax structures. Such a claim, even if proven, would not negate our central conclusions however. The process of determining the means of financing is, in fact, a two step process. Governments will utilize tax institutions which have the most favorable effects on those secondary variables which, in turn, will directly affect voters' perceptions of utility and hence voting decisions.

For example, government may feel the need to reduce the level of aggregate demand in order to control an inflationary pressure and provide price stability if it is to retain office. This reduction may, of course, be implemented through a variety of different policies involving a number of different tax and expenditure institutions. Each of these alternatives will have different implications for vote maximization as seen by the government. It will be an appraisal of these vote implications rather than normative principles that will be of the greatest importance in the choice among alternatives. Vote maximization underlies both the decision of government as to the necessity of providing price stability and the decision as to the appropriate means of doing so.

UNITED STATES' TAX STRUCTURE

We have made a number of predictions as to the outcome to be expected from governmental determination of tax burdens in a society with representative government. Let us now take the United States as an example and examine its tax structure in terms of the "optimal" one we have outlined above. The evidence is by no means irrefutable proof of the validity of our predictions, but the similarities between this structure and the predicted one cannot be ignored.[1] Further work is required before any concrete conclusions can be drawn.

Corporate Taxes

As corporations became the dominant form of organization for firms, producers lost the ability to vote as producers. In proprietorships and partnerships, producers were physical individuals holding dual roles. As corporations became increasingly important, producers became legal as opposed to physical persons and hence they lost whatever voting ability they had. We might expect to see an increase in the taxes placed on corporations and the business sector as this trend continued, and indeed we can see that corporate income taxes rose substantially throughout the first part of this century. (To be sure, there were unusual peaks in tax rates during major wars.) Our optimal tax strategy of government implied that this taxation of corporations was a wise choice because corporations did not vote, and because it would be met with limited resistance since it could be passed forward to consumers.

There is no really conclusive evidence on the degree of shifting of corporate taxes in the U.S. There seems to be a certain amount of agreement among analysts of the problem that there is at least some shifting in certain industries. The opinions range from very limited to extremely high levels of shifting in the short run. Krzyzaniak and Musgrave probably occupy the highest position on this scale. In their pioneering work on the problem of tax shifting they analyzed data for the U.S. in both the pre- and post-World War II years. In their model, shifting, measured in terms of rates of return on total capital, passed

---

[1] Of course, any statistics on the impact of taxation must be taken with a grain of salt. There is really no accurate statistical picture of the world in the absence of taxes, and hence there is no standard against which to measure the post-tax incidence. For example, the granting of tax-free status to income from municipal bonds may lead individuals to purchase them at a yield which is below the market level for taxable bonds. The reduction in pre-tax income that results should really be included in the tax burden of these individuals, but it is presently not possible to do so. Analyses of tax burdens and their distributions are by no means absolutely accurate. They are estimates and should be regarded as such.

134% of the tax forward to consumers.[2] These figures applied to the manufacturing sector only, and are surprisingly high. Their conclusions have not met with universal acceptance by any means, and a number of papers have been published criticizing both the methods and the results.[3]

Some critical authors have made estimates of their own and reached different conclusions regarding the nature and extent of shifting. Kilpatrick's analysis reached the conclusion that the degree of tax shifting over the short run is directly correlated with the degree of concentration in the industry. Those industries with the highest levels of concentration will exhibit the greatest amount of shifting.[4] The most critical of all reject the proposition that there is significant degree of shifting in manufacturing as a whole. Gordon used a mark-up model of producer pricing behavior and examined data for the same general period used by Krzyzaniak and Musgrave. He concluded that there was really no evidence of massive short run shifting and felt that he had disproved much the earlier work.[5] Even he admitted that there was evidence of shifting in highly concentrated industries.

> While tests for each of ten two-digit manufacturing industries reveals no evidence of tax shifting on the average, the industry tax shifting coefficients vary over a considerable range and are significantly correlated with industry concentration ratios.[6]

He also points out that there may indeed be long run shifting in the corporations as a group since his data apply only to short-run effects.

To the extent that shifting is present, corporate income taxes which are nominally progressive in their impact become, in effect, regressive sales taxes. The regressivity is introduced in a highly invisible form while the progressivity is highly visible. The use of such a tax

[2] Marion Krzyzaniak and R. Musgrave, The Shifting of the Corporation Income Tax, Johns Hopkins Press, Baltimore, 1963.

[3] Cf. M. Krzyzaniak, editor, Effects of the Corporation Income Tax, Wayne State University Press, Detroit, 1966. See especially the papers by R. Goode and R. E. Slitor and the Comments and Rejoinder by the above, Krzyzaniak and Musgrave.

[4] R. W. Kilpatrick, "The Short Run Forward Shifting of the Corporation Income Tax," in Yale Economic Essays, Fall 1965, pp. 355–420.

[5] R. J. Gordon, "The Incidence of the Corporation Income Tax in U.S. Manufacturing, 1925–56," in American Economic Review, September 1967, pp. 731–758.

[6] Ibid., p. 733.

strategy in finance fits in with the predicted outcome of decisions made by a vote maximizing government in our model.

Personal Taxes

On the basis of our theory we would also have been able to predict the divergence between nominal and effective tax rates for individuals. The nominal rates of taxation on income range from 14% on incomes below $500 up to a maximum of 70% on all incomes greater than $100,000. However, the standard deduction and exemption lower taxable income for all individuals and hence reduce effective rates. Moreover, there are a number of special provisions which not only lower effective rates, but reduce the progressivity of the tax structure. The effective rate of tax on incomes reaches a maximum of less than 30% at income levels around $200,000 and actually falls to approximately 27% for incomes in excess of $1,000,000. The discrepancies between actual and nominal rates stem from the presence of a number of consciously included loopholes which tend to favor the very wealthy. The regressivity at the upper end of the income scale is largely attributable to capital gains provisions limiting the tax rate on appreciated assets, but also arises due to income splitting and deduction policies.[7]

In addition, there is evidence that a significant number of individuals at the very peak of the income distribution are able to arrange their assets so that they effectively pay no tax at all. It is important to note in the context of our model that all of the tax concessions for the wealthy are accompanied by a justification which can influence consumers' perceptions. For example, oil depletion allowances are justified as being necessary for new oil exploration rather than as necessary to reduce the progressivity of the income tax.

The regressivity of the total tax burden arises in part from the conversion of corporate taxes into sales taxes, but the strongest contributions to regressivity are made by state and local tax institutions.[8] These often consist of sales taxes and real property taxes which hit middle- and lower-income individuals harder than upper-income ones. A recent study by H. P. Miller claims that the combined impact of taxes

---

[7] Cf. Joseph Pechman, *Federal Tax Policy*, Brookings Institution, Washington, D.C., 1966, pp. 65–67; and Pechman, "The Rich, the Poor, and the Taxes they Pay," in *Public Interest*, Fall 1969, No. 17, pp. 21–43.

[8] Pechman, "The Rich . . . ," *op. cit.*, pp. 31–32.

in state, local, and federal programs is such that the very poor pay 50% of their incomes (exclusive of welfare payments) in taxes.[9] The proportion paid by individuals higher up in the income distribution falls substantially.

Pechman has noted this heavy regressivity in the effective tax burden, and has proposed a series of reforms in the federal tax program designed to increase the progressivity of taxes without reducing the level of total revenues generated by taxation. Yet he concludes that such reforms will not be taken because of political as opposed to economic considerations.

> Congress could, if it wishes, increase the yield of the present tax system by $25 billion a year, an amount that would be sufficient substantially to relieve the tax burdens of the poor and low-income nonpoor and to lower tax rates clear across the board. Instead, the revenue to be gained from this year's tax reform bill—a Herculean effort by past standards—may be in the neighborhood of $3 billion a year and much of this will be used to reduce the taxes of the "middle" income classes by what amounts to little more than a pittance, while the poor continue to bear much heavier tax burdens.[10]

Moreover, he concludes that the reduction in tax burdens of the middle income classes is largely due to a "tax revolt" which is caused by the high visibility of their tax burdens. Middle-income individuals "probably pay a smaller proportion of their income in taxes than the poor and near poor, but the taxes they have been paying, or recently began to pay, are highly visible."[11]

Neither the level of overall regressivity in the total tax structure nor the resistance to changing it, even within Congress, can be explained in terms of the normative principles of taxation. Taxes are not distributed in accordance with either ability-to-pay or benefits—they are determined by a political process where those with the greatest incentive and ability to influence taxes actively participate in their own self-interest. We need to consider the political behavior of agents as well as their market behavior before we can come to a rational explanation of the presence and the continuance of this type of tax structure. As Pechman notes once again, the regressivity of taxes is not the result

[9] "The Poor's Heavier Tax Load," *San Francisco Chronicle*, March 19, 1971, p. 5.

[10] Pechman, *op. cit.*, "The Rich . . . ," p. 41.

[11] *Ibid.*, p. 32.

of a normative decision made by consumers acting collectively. It is, instead, the result of different groups exerting different pressures on an uncertain, and hence easily influenced government.

> Of course these actions reflect the pressures on the Congressmen. The influence of the groups arrayed against a significant redistribution of the tax burden is enormous, and there is no effective lobby for the poor and near poor.[12]

CONCLUSIONS

Governments desire office and hence act in a manner aimed at maximizing their votes. They are uncertain as to the best means of doing this, however, and are therefore subject to the influence of selectively priced information in the determination of tax burdens. They will also be susceptible to influence in the form of resources traded for favorable tax policies. We can draw several conclusions about the behavior to be expected of government in this setting.

1. Due to uncertainty, governments will be subject to several types of influence. These include (a) voting, (b) information on voter preferences, (c) information on the effects of alternative policies, and (d) resources to be used by the government in influencing voters' behavior.

2. The greater the degree of uncertainty on the part of the government with regard to voter preferences, the greater its susceptibility to types (a) and (b). The greater its uncertainty as to the reactions of agents to the direct effects of policies, the greater its susceptibility to type (c), and the greater the degree of uncertainty of voters as perceived by government, the greater its susceptibility to type (d). The more uncertainty that is present in the system as a whole, and the higher are the costs of acquiring information, the more likely it is that the solution to the tax distribution problem will be based upon selectively biased information.

3. With uncertainty and the possibility of influence, there exists an optimal overall tax strategy for government which is independent of both of the usual normative principles. This strategy includes the use of nominal progressivity in the form of taxes on producers and high-income people. It includes a reduction in the effective

[12] *Ibid.*, p. 43.

rate of all taxpayers, but does not include subsidizing the information that others have also received effective tax reductions. The progressivity of the tax will be diminished in response to direct political action taken by upper-income individuals which cannot be countered by rational low-income individuals. Finally, the increase in regressivity this necessitates will be implemented by using tax institutions with extremely low visibility.

4. There also exist nontax forms of finance which a government may use to pay for collective expenditures. These include the printing of new money and the issuance of new debt. The choice between these as options, and between nontax and direct tax means of financing will be based upon vote maximization. In our uncertain model, there is no reason to assume that this implies utility maximization.

5. The rational behavior of self-interested agents in an uncertain world reduces the normative benefit and ability-to-pay approaches to taxation to matters of intellectual curiosity. Taxes, in reality, must be determined by the positive "ability-to-influence" principle.

CHAPTER 11
THE IMPACT
OF THE ENTIRE
FISCAL PROGRAM

It is the combined effect of taxes and expenditures which is really important in determining the net impact of governmental action on the distribution of wealth and income in a society. In Part II we held taxes constant and discussed the determination of spending programs; in Part III we have reversed this and examined the determination of the tax structure while holding spending constant. It is the interaction of the two that is of the greatest importance for us in our understanding of the effects of governmental action but, unfortunately, data on the nature of this net effect is quite limited. What little empirical evidence there is seems to be found in the work of W. I. Gillespie.[1]

He attempts to estimate the total tax burden of different income classes, using data on state, local and federal taxes. Similarly, he estimates the distributions of the benefits among different income classes. In both cases the scarcity of good data made it necessary to utilize hypotheses to determine the value of several crucial variables, e.g., he assumes that one-third of the value of the corporation income tax is shifted forward. On the basis of his estimations he reaches some conclusions regarding the actual net impact of fiscal actions in the United States:

> In the broadest terms: (1) the middle income brackets pay the cost of providing themselves with government services: (2) redistribution occurs from the upper income brackets to the lower income brackets, but not in the middle income brackets.[2]

In other words, Gillespie finds that the net impact of fiscal actions is mildly progressive.

There are, however, certain limitations to his analysis which lead us to question this result. The first, and perhaps most serious, one

---

[1] W. Irwin Gillespie, "Effect of Public Expenditures on the Distribution of Income," in R. Musgrave (ed.), *Essays in Fiscal Federalism*, Brookings Institution, Washington, D.C., 1965, pp. 122–186.

[2] *Ibid.*, p. 166.

centers around his assumption that the pre-tax distribution of earnings is unaffected by the fiscal program. In our discussion of public purchasing, we concluded that a number of items will be purchased not for the direct benefit of consumers, but for the benefit of producers. Particularly with regard to the distributions of profits among different firms and industries, and hence to the owners of these firms, pre-tax income is very much dependent upon governmental actions. This is also true in the case of policy decisions that protect the market positions of firms, e.g., import quotas. These effects of fiscal policies were central to our analysis, and hence should be considered in empirical studies used to test it.

Gillespie notes this shortcoming and two others that he feels are unavoidable. He recognizes the arbitrariness of hypothesizing about the degree of shifting of corporate taxes, etc., and he also recognizes the lack of precision in much of his data. A limitation from the standpoint of our analysis that he does not mention is the relatively low value of his highest income category. His top income group consists of households with incomes of $10,000 and above. The studies of tax incidence discussed above point to a regressivity in taxes which appears above $200,000 income levels. An explicit consideration of the net impact of fiscal action on groups in this range would be beneficial in attempting to estimate the net burden on the very wealthy. We have intimated, and in the next section will state explicitly, that we expect the net impact of fiscal actions to reflect the distributions of wealth in a society. Gillespie's findings appear to refute this claim on the surface, but the assumptions he has made and the nature of his data make his conclusions far from undeniable. More empirical work is necessary before any conclusions can be reached, and this work should keep in mind the function of governmental actions in determining the initial distributions of income. Some agents will gain significantly from the entry of government into the market in the form of increased income resulting directly from purchase payments, rather than from the utility derived from government programs. This aspect of fiscal action should be explicitly considered. To be sure, the data necessary for such a study are not currently available, but until they are, we can neither refute nor prove our assertion of wealth affecting the formulation of fiscal policy on empirical grounds.

PART
IV
NON-VOTING
INFLUENCE

INTRODUCTION

> There are no necessary evils in government. Its evils exist only in its abuses. If it would confine itself to equal protection, and, as Heaven does its rain, shower its favors alike on the high and the low, the rich and the poor, it would be an unqualified blessing.
>
> Andrew Jackson

Throughout the first three parts of this paper we have continually spoken of the influence which groups of agents use to affect the actions of other agents. We have claimed that, in a world of uncertainty, much of this influence will be successful in both the political and economic activities of men. It is time to examine this proposition more carefully, particularly in regard to the role influence plays in the determination of governmental policies. The role of votes in this determination is an aspect of behavior which is accepted by the most orthodox theorists. We have included a number of forms of influence which are based upon non-voting behavior. We have intimated that not only do these influences exist, but that they are of much greater importance in determining the actual outcome of public policy decisions than votes themselves.

Government, we have seen, will by necessity be uncertain as to what it should do with regard to voters' preferences, and what it is actually doing. Voters are uncertain as to the need and effectiveness of governmental actions. Into this sea of uncertainty agents may introduce currents of influence which do not consist of votes, but which are of immense importance in setting the course of government.

In general, there are two basic types of non-voting influence used to alter governmental decisions; the first involves the selective pricing and subsidization of information acquired by government and the second involves the implicit or explicit trade of real resources for favorable decisions. Within these two general categories of non-voting influence there exist a vast number of forms which influence can assume. We shall begin by examining a number of these. The second task to be undertaken in this Part is to attempt to outline the process by which agents will choose among the various types and forms as they strive to affect public decisions. We do this by drawing an analogy with choice of techniques in production theory.

The third area to be considered centers around the question of who will be able to engage profitably in influencing activity. To this point we have implicitly assumed a sort of "political perfect competition" where all agents have the opportunity to affect decision making. In this third area we will reconsider this assumption in more explicit terms and attempt to predict which agents will in fact be able to engage rationally in influence either as individuals or as part of a collective group. In the face of this examination we shall have to reject the assumption of perfect competition and conclude instead that decisions will reflect the interests of particular groups in a system such as ours whenever there is a large measure of inequality in the "size" of economic agents.

CHAPTER 12
FORMS OF
NON-VOTING
INFLUENCE

There is no more independence in politics than there is in jail.

Will Rogers

Government faces a production function for votes which depends upon the programs it initiates and the information it provides to voters. Governmental actions can be influenced either by altering the perceptions of government as to the vote producing impact of potential programs or by increasing its ability to provide information to voters in its attempts to alter their perceived utility. Different combinations of program inputs and informational inputs into this production function will yield specific amounts of votes. Influence is aimed at affecting the inputs available to government, or at altering government's perceptions of the production relationship. We have discussed the many forms of non-voting influence that are available to agents in our uncertain system several times in the earlier pages of this work. We shall do no more here than attempt to summarize the various forms and place them into two major categories.

INFORMATION SUBSIDIZATION

Government is driven by a desire to maximize votes in our model and hence it will choose from among its various alternatives the one which yields the greatest expected increase in its net vote position. The key word here is "expected," as one might be able to surmise from the underlining. As we have stated many times, governments are uncertain as to the utility of voters with respect to various programs and hence are not certain as to the vote response they will get from various decisions. Since information as to utility functions is expensive, and rather unreliable as well, governments are susceptible to subsidized information as to the relative intensities of consumer desires. They are also susceptible to information, provided at a subsidized cost, that outlines the ramifications to be expected from the implementation of various programs, and the impact of these developments on voting behavior. A number of different forms of influence fall into this general category.

Informational Lobbying

Much of the pressure placed upon government and its agencies takes the form of freely provided "objective" studies showing the important outcomes to be expected from the enactment of particular policies. This may either be in favor of or against the measures in question. In some cases, this involves providing officials with literature (at the expense of the lobbying group) which either stresses the intensity with which voters care about a given issue or stresses the obviously beneficial (in terms of votes) results to be expected. We can include in this category such activities as providing Congressional testimony.

An example of this type of influence can be seen in the historical example of the debate which raged over the nominal progressivity of income tax structures. On the one hand, the House Ways and Means Committee heard its Special Tax Study Committee decry the progressivity of taxes as a cause of impending economic disaster, a situation unlikely to prove beneficial in terms of votes. This impartial Committee, consisting of a group of "prominent industrialists, bankers and tax lawyers"[1] (none of whom we could expect to have any interest in reduced progressivity, of course) reported to Congress:

> Our country has grown great by the chances we have offered to every country boy and workingman to build himself up by his industry and thrift to as good a position as his capabilities justify. Our great productivity results from the work of men who have made their own ways to the top. [But with the] present scale of tax rates, we have put the brake on men's incentives to a dangerous degree by piling heavier and heavier burdens on them as they try to climb up the ladder. Not only is this stultifying to the kind of dynamic long-term growth that has characterized this country in the past, but—to the extent that it impedes production—it is an element in our inflationary pressures today. [Moreover we now have the] builder who doesn't build the extra house, the farmer who doesn't market the extra carload of cattle or grain, and the wage

[1] Louis Eisenstein, *The Ideologies of Taxation*, The Ronald Press, New York, 1961, p. 57.

earner who doesn't put in the extra day, because doing so would put him in a higher bracket and multiply his tax.[2]

These conditions outlined by the Special Committee in 1947 presented a picture of society which, if realized, would not be beneficial to those seeking re-election. This Committee subsidized the acquisition of certain information by Congress, though it apparently felt it unnecessary to mention the effects on voting from increasing the real tax burdens of lower-income voters, of whom there are many.

In this particular instance the use of informational lobbying was not limited to advocates of a particular position. There were those who at times provided a different picture of progressivity. Six years prior to the report of the Special Committee, the Secretary of the Treasury, attempting to raise sufficient revenues to finance a major war, told the same House Committee that taxation must be based upon the ability to pay if fairness was to be maintained. "The job before us is so big that all the American people must help to carry it out, in proportion to their ability to pay."[3] He, on the other hand, made no mention of the detrimental effects this might have upon the incentives of country boys trying to make good, and through them the effects on the success of the war effort. Influencers will provide only that information which leads toward the "appropriate" conclusion.

On occasion, informational lobbying of government may actually be paid for by consumers, even though they may not actually wish to. To the extent that bureaucrats and bureaucratic agencies engage in actions designed to influence governmental decisions, and to the extent these activities are financed by tax payments, consumers may find themselves paying to have their purchases of particular programs increased. Such a situation is not unheard of. Senator Fulbright claims that the Pentagon engages in extensive and expensive efforts to provide Congress with information as to the necessity, reliability, and desirability in terms of votes of particular military programs. The U.S. Army has a program it calls "Operation Understanding" in which it takes influential citizens on tours of military installations in an effort to impress them with the efficiency and necessity of the military's operation.[4] Ful-

---

[2] The Report of the Special Committee is quoted in Eisenstein, *op. cit.*; the section quoted here comes from page 58 in that work. He discusses the practice of providing information to government more fully in Chapter 4.

[3] Quoted in Eisenstein, *op. cit.*, p. 23.

[4] J. William Fulbright, *The Pentagon Propaganda Machine*, Vintage Books, New York, 1971, pp. 7–9, 34, 78–79.

bright also notes the proclivity of the Defense Department (a branch of the bureaucracy in our framework) to provide classified briefings to members of Congress from districts which will be directly affected by proposed spending programs.[5] In any of these cases, the use of informational lobbying required the spending of significant amounts by the influencer. Influence production, like the production of any other commodity, is not a costless process.

Right To Assembly and Demonstration

Throughout the history of democratically organized states, groups of people who feel they have grievances against the government have been granted the right to gather in order to petition the government for redress of their grievances. In essence, these demonstrations have two roles. First, they provide government with information as to the presence of a certain situation and the degree to which a number of voters object to it. Presumably, individuals willing to demonstrate openly against some policy have a strong relative preference regarding that issue. Secondly, the demonstration may be a method of subsidizing other voters' acquisitions of information as to the existence and efficiency of particular governmental actions. If the process of demonstrating raises the intensity with which nondemonstrating voters view the issue in question, and if the participants in the action are able to convince government that this change in preferences will occur, the influence of demonstrations can far exceed that to be expected on the basis of the number of direct participants.

Demonstrations involve significant costs for the people who engage in them, either in the form of time inputs or in the form of resource costs of organization, implementation, and perhaps legal defense.

Public Opinion Polls

Another form of influence which involves informational pricing to a significant degree is the use of privately commissioned public opinion polls. Sophisticated use of sampling techniques and the appropriate phrasing of questions can cause a poll to reach nearly any conceivable conclusion. Nevertheless, they can act as a fairly accurate representation of the desires and feelings of large numbers of people at any given

[5] *Ibid.*, p. 5.

point in time if these biases are not introduced. Polls are expensive, however, and hence government may be susceptible to polls of limited accuracy which are provided to them free of direct charge. To the extent that they are unable to perceive either the degree or direction of bias, polls of this type will introduce systematic biases into the decision-making process.

The bias that results will be even more pronounced when the results of polls which turn out to be detrimental to specific ends are not provided to government, i.e., the price of unfavorable information is made relatively high with respect to favorable information. Finally, there is usually room for a certain amount of interpretation of the results of polls, and here again, if the subsidized statistics are accompanied by appropriate low cost explanation and summation, their impact can be increased.

Correspondence Campaigns

A fourth form of informational influence takes the form of correspondence campaigns. These may either be based on individual action, or alternatively they may be based on the coordinated activity of a large group. They may use letters, telegrams, postcards, or even phone calls. Their goal is to provide government with free information as to the numbers of people concerned with particular issues and the intensity with which these people care about the outcome. The effectiveness of letters, etc., is increased by the fact that it is really irrational to incur the costs of writing government on most issues so that a small amount of mail implies a much greater degree of support and awareness.

Public Opinion Campaigns

A two-part form of influence production depends upon providing *both* consumers and government with low cost, selective information. A group with a particular policy goal in mind may incur the costs of lowering the price of favorable information to consumers as a group and at the same time provide government with information as to the new intensity of consumers' desires.

The actions of the Army in "Operation Understanding" fall within this type of influence category. By selecting influential civilians to go on "informational" tours, the Army hoped to provide a base of support for military activities among voters.[6] Another example of this type of strategy can be found in the two-part campaign of the National Rifle Association in its efforts to prevent the enactment of gun registration laws. Vast numbers of bumper stickers appeared telling the electorate that "When guns are outlawed only outlaws will have guns."[7] There were also a number of magazine ads and representatives of the NRA on television talk shows proclaiming the right and necessity of maintaining an armed populace. At the same time, there was a strong lobbying effort in Congress pointing to the numbers of people who were becoming increasingly concerned over this issue. There may also have been hints of changes in campaign contributions that could be expected if gun control were enacted.

Similarly, student response to the Cambodian invasion in the spring of 1971 centered around a double strategy. Actions were aimed at increasing the awareness of large numbers of voters of the implications of such activity on the part of the military and, secondly, they were aimed at letting government know of the intensity with which increasing numbers of voters viewed this issue.

There are other forms of informational influence activities than the five mentioned here. All of these forms center around a single fact that must be considered in a positive analysis of governmental decision making, i.e., that voting for representatives provides no real revelation and aggregation of consumers' preferences. This must be done by using non-voting means. All these forms of influence are means by which agents attempt to do this, but rational self-interest requires that they seek to lead government to specific conclusions by revealing only selective information.

CONTROL OVER RESOURCES

The second major category of influence plays upon a different aspect of the uncertainty facing individuals in the economic and political system we have been considering—namely, the uncertainty of consumers as to the actions that governments undertake in the public sphere and the ramifications of these actions, and the actual utility of consumption

---

[6] Cf. Fulbright, op. cit., for a more extensive discussion of this practice.

[7] There are certain tautological aspects of this statement that render it true but trivial. If guns are indeed outlawed, then every person who owns one is by definition an outlaw on the basis of that act alone.

arising from publicly provided goods. As we have seen in the earlier sections of this book, election to office requires significant expenditures on the part of political parties to subsidize consumers' acquisition of favorable information. Because of the high level of uncertainty faced by consumers and the high costs of reducing this uncertainty, most voting decisions will be based upon subsidized information. The party best able to use information in this manner stands the best chance of election. This information is typically designed to increase the utility which individuals expect parties to provide if elected, or, to increase the perceived utility of programs which have already been instituted by the party in power. But, no matter what the content of the information provided, there are real and often very substantial costs incurred by the party providing it. As we noted in an earlier section, a certain amount of these costs may be passed on to the taxpayer by the party in power as a portion of the price of effective government. Nevertheless, much of the costs (all of them for parties out of power) must be met with resources provided by members of the private sector. Since these resources cannot be confiscated and since we have assumed that each individual agent operates in his own self-interest (following such radical economists as Adam Smith), government must offer something of value in exchange for the use of these resources.

Alternatively, since the owners of resources will not wish to reduce their real incomes by arbitrarily giving away some of their wealth, they will only offer them to government when they anticipate a response which yields a net increase in that real income. As in the case of information pricing, there are a number of forms of influence which fall into this major category.

Overt Trading

The most obvious, and hence least desirable from the point of view of vote maximization, takes the shape of an overt trade of resources for political favors. The resource offered here need not go even directly for influencing voters but may instead merely enrich the politician. This obviously falls into the category of bribery, but then bribery is not totally absent from the real world. Despite assurances of complete honesty in government, Bobby Bakers do occasionally appear, "slush" funds are occasionally discovered, and special favors are occasionally granted in response to "unsolicited contributions and gifts."

Because of the dangers of scandal which accompany activities of this type, they are probably limited in usage. Moreover, there are other forms of resource utilizing influence which can be equally effective without running the risk of scandal.

Campaign Financing

No candidate in a modern democracy such as the United States can hope to attain national office without expending vast sums of money in political campaigns. Very few candidates possess sufficient wealth to bear these costs individually. Most are dependent upon the wealth of others to finance their pursuit of power. Therefore, since we have specified that parties formulate policies in order to get elected rather than vice versa, we must conclude that they formulate policies which will be appealing to those individuals who have resources to contribute toward election costs

The direction of motivation in this process of trading is unclear, and it is likely that it operates simultaneously in both directions. Certain contributors may actually propose policy positions to candidates, particularly with respect to the treatment of specific interests, e.g., oil depletion allowances, favorable treatment of labor, etc., in exchange for the promise of campaign funds. On the other hand, certain owners of resources enjoy privileged positions as a direct result of governmental action, and a prerequisite for maintaining this position may be a significant amount of contributions to campaigns. Much of the initial financing of George Wallace's campaign for the Presidency in 1968 is alleged to have come from those who desired the contracts for state construction programs in Alabama, and from those who enjoyed control over the state liquor monopoly.[8]

However, influence of this sort need not be so conspiratorial to be effective. All that is necessary is that a party or a candidate be able to identify certain issues that are of extreme importance to potential contributors. It will then adopt the positions it feels are favorable to these contributors in an effort to attract the resources they control, despite the position deemed optimal by other consumers even if they constitute a majority. *If the resources are sufficient to underwrite the*

[8] Cf. Lewis Chester, G. Hodgson, and B. Page, *An American Melodrama,* Viking Press, New York, 1969, pp. 272–275.

costs of providing enough information to consumers at zero direct price that these consumers also support the party, then this implicit type of "resource influence" will be effective.

If resources are distributed equally among various interests in the system, then there will be no inherent bias resulting from this behavior. If, however, resources are distributed with a significant degree of inequality, and if there are identifiable interests common to those at the top of this distribution, then government must adhere to the policies desired by these interests. Parties seeking office who neglected these interests could expect to see substantial amounts of resources going to competitors in order to insure the defeat of the "renegade" parties. To some observers this process is so binding that the largest agents in the system will effectively dictate policy. (In a country such as the United States, corporations are without question the largest economic agents.)

> This does not mean, of course, that the business community as such must prefer a particular candidate or party for that candidate or party to be victorious. It means, more fundamentally, that short of committing political suicide, no party or government can step outside the framework of the corporate system and its politics and embark on a course which consistently threatens the power and privileges of the giant corporations.[9]

To the extent that this is true, the policy positions of parties and government will depend upon the distribution of economic power rather than the distribution of votes.

Such a conclusion would not be of trivial importance. Carried to its extreme, some analysts of political behavior claim that election to office is becoming solely the result of efficiently managed campaigning—campaigning which depends upon the control of real resources. Speculating about the future of Presidential elections in the U.S., James Perry foresees carefully controlled programs of sampling with polls and then presentations of appropriate information to each subgroup of voters.

> And the candidate? He will be out front, moving with a robot-like precision, being fed with data from the polls and the simulator. He will no doubt be articulate, and probably will be handsome and vigorous. And

---

[9] David Horowitz (ed.), *Corporations and the Cold War*, Modern Reader, New York, 1969, pp. 12–13.

he may or may not be qualified to be the next President of the United States.[10]

If this is truly the case, or even an approximation of it, then the ability to provide resources carries with it immense power to influence political decisions. If the distribution of wealth and political interests coincide, then government policy must reflect this distribution. There need be no distinct contact between politicians and influencers for this to be effective. There is at work in such a situation an "invisible hand" moving toward this end, though it is not exactly the same hand envisioned by Adam Smith.

Opinion Leaders

A final form of influence centers around a number of individuals who control more than their own single votes. These may be along the lines of Downs' "agitators" or they may simply enjoy celebrity status or institutional importance. For example, Frank Sinatra often endorses political candidates and this endorsement is presumably worth some votes. Indeed, one of the more closely watched and interesting aspects of the 1972 Presidential campaign was the "celebrity race" to see who could gather into their camp more big names from show business and sports. Similarly, the leaders of the major labor unions can influence large blocs of votes by endorsing candidates to their memberships. These individuals thus control a valuable and scarce resource which is not significant in other aspects of society—they control votes. These individuals may then affect governmental policy decisions, either through implicit or explicit promises of support. Alternatively, opinion leaders may exert negative pressure by threatening to support opposing parties unless certain policy measures are enacted. In the 1968 Presidential campaign a number of southern leaders reportedly extracted a high price from the Nixon branch of the Republican Party in exchange for their promise not to support Wallace, or even such political newcomers as Ronald Reagan.[11]

Influence is a central factor in the determination of policies in the public realm. It may manifest itself in any number of forms, but it

[10] James M. Perry, *The New Politics: The Expanding Technology of Political Manipulation*, C. N. Potter, 1968, p. 6.
[11] Cf. Chester, Hodgson and Page, *op. cit.*, "Act IX," Parts 3, 4, and 5.

always maintains the central characteristic of attempting to lead public decision makers to choose that alternative most beneficial to the influencing group. It may rely either on the use of information pricing or resource control, but its central role is always the same. Voting cannot be used as an efficient guide to policy decisions. Non-voting influence of several various types can be and hence will be used for this purpose. There are real costs involved in the use of any of these forms, however, and hence only agents with at least a minimal control over resources will be able to afford its production. Influence is not a free good; it requires substantial expenditures.

CHAPTER 13
CHOICE AMONG ALTERNATE FORMS OF INFLUENCE

There are many different combinations of inputs that will yield the desired product, and obviously the cheapest combination will maximize the producer's profits.

George Stigler

The more abundant the supply of any productive factor, compared to the supplies of other factors, the relatively cheaper will be that factor.

Delbert A. Snider

Any individual or group in our system which perceives an opportunity to realize a net gain through influencing public decisions is faced with the entire array of influence forms outlined in the previous section as well as many others. If we maintain our assumption of rational behavior for all agents, then the choice among these different forms of influence will not result from a purely random selection process, but will instead follow certain distinct patterns. Each agent whose *ex ante* estimates indicate the profitability of producing influence will utilize those forms which are, in some sense, most efficient given his initial resource endowments. Borrowing terminology from the field of international trade, we may say that agents will use those forms of influence which relatively intensively use those influence-producing factors with which they are most abundantly endowed. The exact meaning of this statement will become clearer as we proceed.

It is obvious from the above that we intend to examine the choice of influence forms in the context of production theory. The problem at hand is completely analogous to the choice of production techniques when a number of alternate methods are available. The product in this case is "influence" and the producer is the agent who engages in "influencing" activities.

We shall beg the question of arbitrating among the various definitions of influence which have been offered by political theorists and instead provide a definition of our own which fits in our positive system. The production of influence as we have discussed it involves attempts by agents to increase their real incomes by altering relevant decisions made in the public sphere. It should be possible to quantify this change in real income brought about by these actions and call the resultant figure "influence." This figure will not, by our definition, be a net figure, but will merely record the gross alteration in real income to be expected from engaging in the various activities outlined previously. To arrive at a net figure it will be necessary to subtract the costs of influence which, in many cases, will be quite substantial. As a result, even though the gross return from any of these activities will be assumed to be positive, the net return to influence-producing activities may be negative.

Let us put the problem into more rigorous terms by defining an influence function:[1]

$$I = I(f_1, f_2, f_3, \ldots f_n) \tag{1}$$

where I is the gross influence produced measured in money terms and the f_i represent the levels of activity using each of the possible influence-producing forms. We can then go a step further by assuming that all inputs into these activities can be reduced to time inputs, T, and resource inputs, R. We can then define a series of functions

$$f_i = f_i(T_i, R_i) \quad \text{where} \quad i = 1, 2, \ldots n \tag{2}$$

one for each of the n possible techniques of production. T_i is the total time input into activity i and R_i is the total resource input into the same activity. Time and Resources are the primary factors of production in our theory of the production of political influence. We assume that the partial derivatives of (2) are both positive.

We can now substitute (2) into (1) in order to get

$$I = I[f_1(T_1, R_1), f_2(T_2, R_2), \ldots f_n(T_n, R_n)]$$

which we can reduce to the new function

$$I = I'(T, R). \tag{3}$$

---

[1] As with much of the formal economics done today, the equations and graphs express a relatively simple idea. In order to produce political influence you must have some resource, either time or money. Unless the expected gain to you is greater than the value of the resources used, you won't bother with influence production. The method of influence depends on what type of inputs are relatively easily available to you. In simpler terms yet, what we are saying is that what you can do depends upon what you've got—both in economics and in politics.

We would also expect to find that the partial derivatives of (3) are both positive. This new function, (3), describes the total gross changes in income which are possible using the various production methods available. The decision whether to produce or not is essentially dependent upon the relationship between this function and a cost of influence function

$$C = C(wT, rR, a). \tag{4}$$

Here C is the total cost of producing influence measured in dollar amounts, w is the implicit wage rate which gives the value of time, and r is the price per unit of other resources. The parameter a is included in order to take account of the influence producing activities of others. If the agent in question here expects other agents to produce influence counter to his, then his costs of causing an increase in his gross income rise. If he expects others to engage in supportive influence, the costs fall. The parameter a reflects these expectations. If costs of influence depend upon other things as well, e.g., the lower communications costs of the wealthy in Downs' analysis, this can also be reflected in a.

The problem facing the potential producer is then relatively simple. He wishes to maximize the "profit" or the net increase in his real income from political activity. In terms of the functions specified above, his problem is to

$$\max (I - C)$$

but he is limited in his ability to do this by two constraints

$$R \leq R_o \tag{5}$$

and

$$T \leq T_o \tag{6}$$

where R_o and T_o are the initial resource endowments of primary factor inputs.

The problem essentially consists of two parts; first, is it profitable to produce any influence at all and if so, how much; and secondly, if influence is to be produced, which production technique is optimal? Obviously, the optimal level of production is where $(I - C)$ is actually at the highest potential level, i.e., where $dC/dI = 1$, but whenever it is positive but held at less than a maximum by constraints (5) and (6), some influence is advisable, even if it is less than the optimum amount.

In Figure 1 we have presented a graphical representation of

equations (3) and (4). In the drawing we have assumed a significant initial cost involved in influence production, followed by a period of increasing returns to scale only to be replaced by decreasing returns past some point. We could have used other shapes for the cost function, but any shape, other than the most unorthodox ones, would yield similar results. The dotted curve C_o depicts the cost curve for the same individual when he expects other agents to engage in counter influence production.

Using curve C, we can see that the optimum level of influence production is I_2 where the difference between I and C is maximized. However, there is still a net gain to be realized by producing any amount of influence greater than I_1. If our subject expects counter influence so that C_o is the appropriate curve, then the minimum level of production which will be profitable is I_o. For the remainder of the analysis we shall assume that no counter influence is expected.

Therefore, the ideal position from the point of view of the potential influencer is production at level I_2. However, the ability to

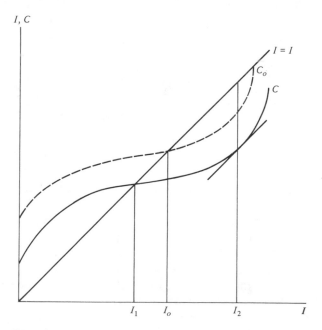

Figure 1

produce influence depends upon the availability of potential inputs into the production process, which in our model implies that the ability to influence will depend upon constraints (5) and (6). The maximum level of production attainable is I_M, where

$$I_M = I'(R_o, T_o) \tag{7}$$

which will be less than I_2 in many cases. If we had perfect capital markets, agents could acquire sufficient current resources to insure the attainment of the optimum level. In the absence of such perfection many agents will be unable to produce the total amount of influence that would be profitable.

Still, as long as $I_1 \leq I_M \leq I_2$, the potential influencer will indeed engage in the production of influence of amount I_M since such activity yields a net benefit to him. However, there are a number of methods by which influence can be produced, i.e., there exists a necessity for choosing the best technique from among those discussed above. A rational agent will make this choice on the basis of his relative endowments of the two inputs into the production process, and upon the opportunity costs he faces with regard to other uses of these inputs. An agent with a relatively high resource endowment will choose production techniques that use resources relatively intensively. Another agent with identical physical endowments, but higher opportunity costs of time will use still more resource-intensive production methods. Other things equal, the resource-intensity of production techniques will increase as the resource endowment increases and as the opportunity cost of time rises.

Since large economic agents have relatively high endowments of resources and often have high opportunity costs for time, we could predict that they will most often utilize these resource-intensive methods. This explains why we seldom see the combined Board chairmen of the Fortune Five Hundred marching on Washington in an attempt to influence policies. Alternatively, very small economic agents, i.e., the poor, generally have low resource endowments and often have low opportunity costs for time (especially when unemployed). We would expect them to use time-intensive approaches to production. This partially explains why we have poor peoples' marches but very few large campaign contributions from poverty groups. Rational agents minimize the costs of producing influence and on this basis choose the techniques to be employed.

The control over resources thus affects the patterns of influence we can expect in two distinct ways. First, a certain minimum control over resources is necessary before influence production can be profitable and, in many cases, this minimum may be quite substantial. Secondly, assuming that influence is feasible with regard to a given issue, the choice of techniques of production will reflect the relative endowments of agents and the opportunity costs they face.

CONCLUSIONS

The rational, self-interested agents who make up our political-economic system will have to determine the optimal strategy, given their estimates of costs and benefits, with regard to the production of influence. There are several aspects to this decision—do the estimates yield an expected net return from such activity that is greater than zero, and if so, at what level should influence be produced; and finally, what methods of production should be utilized? There are several observations we can make with regard to this decision.

1. For those agents whose estimates yield a net gain, the choice of production techniques will be based upon relative resource endowments and opportunity costs. Production inputs can be reduced to "time" and "resource" inputs, and agents who enjoy a relatively high initial endowment of one of these will use methods which relatively intensively use that factor. Similarly, as the opportunity costs of one input rise, the choice will shift away from techniques that use it relatively intensively.
2. It will not be profitable for all agents to engage in the production of influence with regard to all questions. It is apparent that there is a minimum feasible level of production. At any level below this, such activity will yield a net loss.
3. In the absence of perfect capital markets the ability to attain this minimum level depends upon initial endowments of factor inputs relevant to the production of influence.
4. The level of activity which is associated with this minimum will increase with the expectation of counter-influence being produced by other agents in the system. Counter-influence tends to raise the costs of causing a shift in the real income of the first agent and hence increases the value of the minimum level. If the coun-

tering agents enjoy a relatively higher endowment of resources, their achievable gain will be relatively greater, and more activity on their part is to be expected. This will increase both their chances of success and the costs of influence as seen by the original agent.

5. On the basis of these conclusions we could predict that agents with relatively high resource endowments will engage in influence production more often, and at higher levels than those with low endowments. If, as Downs has suggested, there are lower communications costs for wealthier agents, then this tendency toward large economic agents dominating influence production will be reinforced.

Those agents with the largest incentive in terms of the relationship between costs and benefits of influence and the greatest potential in terms of endowments of influence producing factors will be the ones who produce political influence successfully. The decisions of the public sector will reflect this distribution of incentives and abilities.

CHAPTER 14
INFLUENCERS

> Probably the most powerful factor preventing one group from upsetting the balance of power is the existence of other groups. Organization invites counter-organization. The increased influence of one group forces competing groups to strengthen themselves.
>
> **James MacGregor Burns**
> **Jack Walter Peltason**

It seems apparent from the foregoing analysis that on any issue to be decided in the public arena, a single agent with a large endowment of resources will have a distinct advantage over an agent with a smaller endowment and opposing interests. This is so for two reasons. First, the large endowment will allow the agent to produce influence closer to, and perhaps at, the optimum level. Secondly, this production of influence by the wealthier individual agent will serve to raise the costs of production for the other agent, and perhaps raise the minimum level of feasible production to a position that is unattainable with the smaller endowment. Activity by the smaller agent would, of course, also affect the costs of the larger, but it is less likely to make them prohibitive. Agents who enjoy large resource endowments will also enjoy a significant ability to influence public decisions and actions. Agents with less resources will be able to influence less often and less successfully.

It is thus obvious that we would expect to see economically large agents involved in the production of political influence in defense of their positions with little opposition from single small agents. In the face of this conclusion, the question we need to examine in this section is whether or not this excessive power of large agents will be counterbalanced by the actions of small agents acting collectively rather than individually. It is apparent that, on an individual basis, large agents have much more power than small—is this also true in the face of possible collective action by rational, self-interested agents? In seeking the answer to this question, we shall first examine the work of Mancur Olson who analyzes the behavior of rational agents with respect to collective action,[1] and then we shall see what implications this has for the problem of the production of political influence.

[1] Mancur Olson, Jr., *The Logic of Collective Action: Public Goods and the Theory of Groups,* Schocken Books, New York, 1968.

OLSON ON COLLECTIVE ACTION

According to Olson's analysis, the rational behavior of self-interested agents will lead them to voluntarily join a group acting collectively only when certain restrictive conditions are met. His collective bodies are "groups" which consist of individuals, each of whom could benefit from the "production" of some "collective" good. A "collective" good, in this sense, is one which must be provided to all members of a group if it is provided to any. In terms of our system, the collective good could be a change in policy which provides benefits for a number of individual agents. For example, a decision by government to reduce the excise tax on liquor would provide benefits to all purchasers of liquor in the form of lower prices. It is not feasible to lower the taxes paid by some buyers without lowering them for all. If such a good could be provided by a sufficient amount of influence being produced, the question we need to ask of Olson's work is whether liquor consumers will band together and share the costs of such production.

Olson establishes conditions under which we can presume a collective good to be provided. In the absence of these conditions, he concludes that the good will not be provided. Let us examine what these conditions are. He defines a number of variables to be used in his analysis, and in order to minimize confusion, we utilize the same notation here.[2] Let there be some collective good which can be provided at a level T and let there be a cost function $C = C(T)$ which describes the costs of this provision. Olson assumes that there will be significant initial costs and that the average curves will exhibit the traditional U-shape. The size of the "group" which receives benefits from this good is given by S_g and it depends not only on the number of agents in the group, "but also on the value of a unit of the collective good to each individual in the group."[3] V_g is the value of the group gain and V_i is the value of the gain to individual i. The fraction of the gain enjoyed by individual i is given by F_i which is equal to V_i/V_g.

Then for any individual acting alone, we can presume that he will incur the costs of producing the collective good by himself, if that is necessary to insure its production, whenever $F_i > C/V_g$. The gains he receives are sufficiently great that he will provide it himself if he cannot persuade others to share the cost. The optimum amount for him

---

[2] Cf. *Ibid.*, Chapter I, Part D, pp. 22–33.
[3] *Ibid.*, p. 23.

to obtain is one where $F_i\left(\dfrac{dV}{dT}g\right)=\dfrac{dC}{dT}$. Obviously, as the number of individuals in a group increases, the probability of the share of any one of them being sufficiently great to insure provision of the public good decreases, i.e., it is less likely that the highest F_i will exceed C/V_g.

We can thus be less sure that the collective good will be provided as the number of agents in the group grows, particularly if they share the benefits equally. No one agent can afford to provide the good and hence we must rely solely on collective action to meet the costs of provision. Is it likely to occur in larger groups? Olson claims it depends on how much larger the groups is. If it is still small enough that the behavior of one agent has a noticeable impact on the behavior of others, then it is still possible that collective action will occur. This is essentially analogous to the oligopoly situation in market analysis. Olson claims that in a medium size range, strategic activity is probable, and that this strategy will determine whether or not the good is actually provided.

His example is one where a collective good is already being provided and a single individual considers withdrawing his support for the group. In such a situation this individual must be aware that his refusal to continue bearing a portion of the costs will noticeably increase the shares which must be borne by others in the group. Our subject may even be aware that his refusal could prompt enough others to withdraw support from the collective good, from which he is enjoying benefits, to cause its elimination. In such a case his choice cannot be predicted for the situation is ripe for bargaining and the outcome is indeterminate. Collective action may or may not take place.[4]

In very small groups, where the gain to any individual is quite high relative to the costs, a collective good will be provided by rational individuals. As the size of the group increases to the point where no one individual receives enough gain to insure the provision of the good, but where each individual's actions affect others' welfare, the collective good may or may not be provided. The outcome is indeterminate. When the size of the group increases still more, then no individual can afford to provide the good and, moreover, his refusal or willingness to contribute toward the provision of this good in proportion to his own gain will not significantly affect the actions of other agents. In these

4 Cf. Olson, *op cit.*, p. 43.

situations Olson concludes that rational individuals will not voluntarily engage in any collective action.

> ... in a large group in which no single individual's contribution makes a perceptible difference to the group as a whole, or the burden or benefit of any single member of the group, it is certain that a collective good will not be provided unless there is coercion or some outside inducements that will lead the members of the large group to act in their common interest.[5]

This conclusion is based upon the assumed behavior of rational self-interested individuals. It is reinforced by the presence of substantial organizational costs which Olson logically assumes are an increasing function of the number of individuals to be organized. The members of the group will have to bear these costs as well as the costs of actually providing the collective good; as the size of the group increases this added burden will serve to discourage collective action.

> This means that there are now three separate but cumulative factors that keep larger groups from furthering their own interests. First, the larger the group, the smaller the fraction of the total group benefit any person acting in the group interest receives, and the less adequate the reward for group oriented action, and the farther the group falls short of getting an optimal supply of the collective good, even if it should get some. Second, since the larger the group, the smaller the share of the total benefit going to any individual, or to any (absolutely) small subset of the group, the less the likelihood that any small subset of the group, much less any single individual, will gain enough from getting the collective good to bear the burden of providing even a small amount of it; in other words, the larger the group the smaller the likelihood of oligopolistic interaction that might help obtain the good. Third, the larger the number of members in the group the greater the organization costs, and thus the higher the hurdle that must be jumped before any of the collective good at all can be obtained. For these reasons, the larger the group the farther it will fall short of providing an optimal supply of a collective good, and very large groups will not, in the absence of coercion or separate, outside incentives, provide themselves with even minimal amounts of a collective good.[6]

There are a number of important implications this analysis has for the system we have been developing. We can look at governmental decisions as collective goods which pertain to specific groups of people. The means by which these public goods come into being is through

[5] *Ibid.*, p. 44.
[6] *Ibid.*, p. 48.

the process of influence production, and the costs of this production are part of the costs of providing the collective good. We can only be certain that influence will be produced in the case of goods pertaining to small groups of relatively large agents, or perhaps to medium-sized groups of agents in an "oligopolistic" type of situation. It will not, in general, be produced by large numbers of small agents banding together in pursuit of their common interest. For example, we might see a large producer of missile systems engaged in influence production favoring the systems; we would not, on the basis of Olson's work, expect to see consumers, who must pay for the systems, organized to counter this influence. It isn't rational for any one of them to do so, and it isn't even rational for all of them acting as a group to do so.

Only if a degree of exclusion is possible can we expect to see concentrated action on the part of large, collective bodies aimed at producing effective political influence. If the decision is such that only those who belong to the organization and bear a portion of the costs will receive the benefits, the group may function. Even here, however, as the group expands in size the costs of organization may become prohibitive. *Indeed, this is the very reason why government came into existence in the first place in our model—to overcome the irrationality of voluntarily contributing to the costs of providing non-excludable collective goods.* This irrationality remains when we wish to speak of collective action in the production of political influence.

We can now offer an answer to the question posed at the beginning of this section; i.e., whether the excessive power of larger economic agents will be counter-balanced by the actions of small agents acting collectively. That answer must be that we cannot expect such action to take place if we are to maintain our assumptions of rationality and self-interest. The ability to produce influence profitably that accrues to those with substantial initial resource endowments will yield a substantial advantage, particularly when the agents "opposed" to that particular influence are many, and on the average quite small in terms of economic position.

CHAPTER 15
PATTERNS
OF INFLUENCE
PRODUCTION

> Neither current events nor history show that the majority rules, or ever did rule.
>
> **Jefferson Davis**

Voting, it seems, does not provide a means for the expression of the preferences of voters with regard to particular issues in our system. Yet decisions must be, and are, made in the political realm which presumably reflect consumers' preferences in one form or another. These decisions, by necessity in a world of uncertainty, are to be made on the basis of non-voting influence. The patterns which this influence assumes will effectively determine the patterns of governmental decisions and the policies that arise from them. In a world of rational, self-interested agents, these patterns of influence will not arise in a strictly random manner, but will instead reflect the predictable behavior of these agents.

Both the decision whether to produce influence at all, and the decision as to the appropriate techniques of production depend upon the endowments of time and resources agents possess. With regard to a particular issue, those individual agents with the largest incentive in terms of potential return, and the greatest ability in terms of inputs will produce influence. Large economic agents have a substantial advantage in the production of influence over smaller agents. If capital markets were perfect, this advantage might be eliminated, but in the absence of such perfection it will be quite real. The patterns of influence which are produced by individuals will reflect most heavily the political desires of the largest economic agents.

What about collective action which could conceivably counter this tendency? Olson shows that only relatively small groups can rationally engage in group action aimed at providing collective benefits in the absence of some strong non-market incentive or coercion. In terms of government policies this implies that producers who enjoy high market power will have a strong incentive to act individually, or even

155

collectively, to influence public purchasing decisions in their favor. The large numbers and relatively small size of consumers prohibits them from engaging in countering influence production. Economic power in the form of excessive control over resources and markets carries with it the inevitable connotation of excessive political control over governmental decisions. Votes do not determine most specific public decisions, non-voting influences must, and large economic agents have substantially greater ability to produce this influence than their mere numbers would warrant. *Policies will reflect the distribution of economic resources.*

To the degree that inequality exists in the distribution of wealth, it implies inequality in both market and political power distributions. The greater the relative size of an agent in economic terms, the greater his ability to influence. There is no question that General Motors enjoys a greater ability to influence policy issues in a variety of ways than does the independent corner gas station.

It is a basic conclusion of economic theory that the allocation of resources arising from the operation of a market system will reflect the initial distribution of wealth and the structure of the market. It is effective demand which matters, and hence the ability to buy in the form of wealth implies a large influence over resource allocations. It is also the inevitable result of rational, self-interested action on the part of all agents in an uncertain world that the outcome of decisions in the political realm, even when organized democratically, will also reflect this same distribution!

The greater the concentrations of wealth held by any agent, the greater his political power. Gigantic corporations not only possess excessive control over their markets, but they also possess excessive control over governmental decisions. The same applies to extremely wealthy individuals. Moreover, the more complex the society becomes and the more advanced technology increases the isolation of agents from information relevant to the decisions they must make, the greater will be the potential for influence and hence the greater the advantage enjoyed by these large agents. In either the political or the market operations of a society such as the one we have been describing, the wishes of the agents with the greatest wealth will carry the greatest weight. It is not a new "conspiracy" that makes it so. It is merely the action of self-interested rational men.

PART

V

THE
SYSTEM
AND
THE
LONG-RUN
STRUCTURE
OF
SOCIETY

INTRODUCTION

> For the poor always ye have with you.
>
> **John 12:8**

Nearly thirty-five years ago Harold Lasswell defined political science as the study of "who gets what, when, how"; economics could really be defined by the same simple phrase. In his widely used text Samuelson defines economics as the study of how ". . . we choose to use scarce productive sources, with alternate uses, to meet prescribed ends—what goods to produce, how, and for whom, now or later."[1] Economists also seek to know what is produced, who gets it, when they get it and the process by which they get it. In his search for the answer to this problem Lasswell moved from this simple definition to a rather far-reaching analysis of the nature of political states and human society. Yet economists, asking the same questions, tend to arrive at answers on a far different plane than Lasswell's. We tend to take the nature of society as given rather than as an endogenous aspect of models of human behavior.

There is thus some benefit to be gained at this juncture by attempting to push our analysis into a different, and broader, dimension. The experience we have gained in the practice of the economic science may prove valuable in the exploration of this new dimension. Unfortunately, analysis at this level is not yet as "clean" as analysis on the more traditional planes, yet there is still some important insight to be gained by putting society back together rather than persisting in taking it further and further apart. Such a task will be difficult at best, but because of the scarcity of such undertakings, the marginal return may indeed be significant. No magic numbers will be generated, even in symbolic form, which will tell us much about society, but a certain amorphous degree of understanding (something which is not really quantifiable, even conceptually) may result. Such understanding is not without value.

The use of economic resources to produce influence in the fiscal process of a democratically organized state has been examined in some depth in the previous Parts of this book. We have concluded

---

[1] Paul Samuelson, *Economics,* Seventh Edition, McGraw-Hill, New York, 1967, p. 13.

that the actual allocation of resources in an economy with a large governmental sector will reflect the distribution of wealth, both in the outcome of market and of political decisions. We have concentrated so far on the short-run effects of influence production in a society where this distribution and the basic value system are regarded as initially given. In order to reach this new dimension of analysis, it is now necessary to examine the formation of this value system in the form of a national ideology, and its effects upon the distributions of long-run political and economic power.

Our analysis will utilize the framework of observers such as Marx and Lasswell to the extent that we shall divide society into different groups or classes. Our task will be to utilize the positive analysis of political decision making formulated in the earlier parts of this paper to understand some of the relationships between these groups. The relationships are both political and economic in nature. It will be important in this section to distinguish between the types of groupings we have used previously which are based upon market functions, and the more basic groupings which are based upon social and political dominance. In some cases our previous categories may coincide with these new groups, but for the most part they will differ. Short-run market groups function within the wealth distributions and the ideological framework of society which are normally taken as given. They may influence the short-run nature of society by engaging in the activities discussed above. Groups based upon social dominance may use the same basic process of influence production to affect this distribution of wealth and power, and coincidentally, the very ideological framework normally regarded as a fixed constraint. Over the long term, this will be most important in determining "who gets what, when, how."

CHAPTER 16
SOCIAL
STRUCTURE

In every society where property exists there will be a struggle between rich and poor. Mixed in one assembly, equal laws can never be expected; they will either be made by the members to plunder the few who are rich, or by influence to fleece the many who are poor.

John Adams

A sage observer of academia once proclaimed that the world is divided into two types of people, those who feel they must divide the world into two types of people and those who do not. We shall have to place ourselves in the first category in this portion of the book, but in so doing we will find ourselves in the company of a number of reputable analysts. For example, Lasswell claims that every state has a two-part division between those who have more, the "elite," and those who have less, the "mass." For him, societies tend toward inequality in the distribution of such values as "deference, income, and safety" and the "elite" is composed of those individuals who "get the most of what there is to get." Those who share the remainder are known as the mass.[1]

C. Wright Mills visualizes a similar sort of division in society, but his work is more historical than theoretical. He concentrates upon American society in the period following World War II. He attempts to identify and analyze the behavior of those individuals who compose what he terms the "power elite." This group, which tends to represent the interests of wealth, is based upon the ability to control decisions, i.e., power. Certain members of society possess the implicit or explicit authority to make decisions which have serious consequences for the course of American and world history, yet he claims they are effectively isolated from the mass which must often bear the burden of these decisions. Like Lasswell, he sees the world as a place where some individuals have greater wealth and greater power than others, even when

---

[1] For a more complete discussion, see Harold Lasswell, *Politics: Who Gets What, When How,* World Publishing Co., New York, Meridian Books, 1958.

the society in question has a basically democratic form of political organization.[2]

> The owner of a roadside fruit stand does not have as much power in any area of social or economic or political decision as the head of a multimillion-dollar fruit corporation; no lieutenant on the line is as powerful as the Chief of Staff in the Pentagon; no deputy sheriff carries as much authority as the President of the United States. . . .

> By the power elite, we refer to those political, economic and military circles which, as an intricate set of overlapping cliques, share decisions having at least national consequences. Insofar as nationwide events are decided, the power elite are those who decide them.[3]

According to Mills, there will be an inherent bias in the decisions forthcoming from this group—a bias which tends to favor the interests of the social and economic class from which the elite comes when it conflicts with the interests of other classes. The bias need not be the result of an evil conspiracy of oppression; all that is necessary is that the elite be composed of men who, like all humans, view the world from the perspective of their own experiences and knowledge. To the extent the elite comes from a specific type of life style and experience, it will be reflected in their decisions. The "national interest" will often be merely a class interest. If those with the authority to make decisions actually perceive the "business of America to be business," then policy decisions will reflect the desire to protect U. S. investments and the business community because such actions are believed to be in the "national" interest.

There seems to be general agreement among analysts as to the inequality in the ability to affect decisions in modern democratic societies when viewing individuals.[4] However, not all observers would accept Mills' allegation of an inevitable class bias in the outcome of public decisions. For example, Robert Dahl also claims that a central characteristic of political systems, even democratic ones, is an uneven distribution of political influence—certain individuals will always have far more than proportional influence on the formation of policy. Yet for Dahl this does not necessarily imply the presence of biases in the out-

---

[2] C. Wright Mills, *The Power Elite*, Oxford University Press, London, 1956.
[3] *Ibid.*, p. 18.
[4] On occasion, economists have also stressed the unequal distribution of power and its effects in terms of the patterns of public policy decisions. Cf. Vilfredo Pareto, *The Mind and Society*, Harcourt Brace, New York, 1935, especially Vol. III, p. 1569, and Downs, *op. cit.*

come. He adopts a position of "pluralism," claiming that often these powerful individuals will represent divergent points of view and hence the excessive power will tend to be balanced by countervailing power.[5]

Divisions of society into different groups is not a practice which originated with either of these analysts. Well over a century ago Karl Marx looked at society and claimed that it was marked by tensions between those who owned the means of production and those who did not. His analysis revolved around the conflicts of interests between these two classes and the oppression of the proletariat he saw increasing at the hands of capital:

> Society as a whole is more and more splitting up into two great hostile camps, into two great classes facing each other—bourgeosie and proletariat. . . . The executive of the modern state is but a committee for managing the common affairs of the whole bourgeosie.[6]

He would have agreed with Mills' claim of bias in the outcome of decisions made on a national scale.

We shall follow in the footsteps of these and other diverse scholars and divide the society in our model into two general classifications—those who enjoy a disproportionate share of its benefits and those who do not. In a division of this type we can claim no originality, only concurrence. In order to be more precise in this, let us form an index number describing the control each individual in the society has over the essential political and economic "values." We shall include in this index of "values" those items regarded as important in the Lasswellian system: income or wealth, deference and security—rather amorphous qualities to be sure, but ones which are, after all, at least as quantifiable as "utility" and "capital." Let us then rank all individuals according to the value of this index number assigned to them, placing those with the highest numbers on top. We can then draw a line somewhere along this ranking separating the population into two groups. The actual location of the line is of course arbitrary, but all that is really necessary for our analysis is the acceptance of its existence as a conceptual entity.[7]

---

[5] Robert Dahl, *Modern Political Analysis*, Prentice Hall, Englewood Cliffs, New Jersey, 1963, especially Chapters 3 and 4.

[6] Karl Marx and Frederich Engels, *The Communist Manifesto*, Appleton–Century–Crofts, Inc., New York, 1955, pp. 9–12.

[7] This division obviously rests on an implicit assumption that the distribution of values will not be perfectly equal. If perfect equality held, we would

We will borrow Lasswell's terminology and call all of those who lie above this line and hence enjoy a disproportionate share of the society's values the "elite." All those below the line will be termed the "mass." It is important to stress the fact that we intend no normative connotations to accompany the use of these terms. They were chosen for convenience rather than rhetoric. We might easily have used terms such as "more fortunate" and "less fortunate" but found "elite" and "mass" significantly less awkward.

In all probability there will be representatives of all of our previous market classifications among the elite, i.e., the well-to-do will include politicians, consumers, bureaucrats, and producers. No group is specifically rejected from, or limited to, membership in the elite. Certain groups may or may not have disproportionate representation among the elite.

Resorting to admittedly casual empiricism we could predict a few characteristics of this distribution of values and the relative size of the elite when compared to the mass. It seems most likely that the distribution will be skewed toward the top of the scale, implying that a few high "scores" will wield a heavy influence on the mean, raising it above the median. Those with the highest scores will make up the elite, and since we would expect the line dividing it from the mass at least to be equal to the mean value, there will most likely be more individuals in the mass than the elite. This is certainly true with regard to the distributions of wealth in most countries, and while those with the greatest wealth do not always have excessive control of the other values, we would still expect a significant positive correlation.

Inequality in the short-run distribution of values is certainly possible in a democratic society composed of rational individuals pursuing their own self-interest. However, its continuation over extended periods carries with it certain implications regarding the behavior and the perceptions of these agents. If we may oversimplify for a moment and look exclusively at the distribution of wealth (the value most easily quantified), we can see that long-term inequality requires what would appear to be irrational behavior on the part of consumers. As long as there exist individuals whose wealth exceeds the median level for so-

---

not have a distribution at all but merely a single point, and hence it would be impossible to rank and divide individuals. However, we feel confident in predicting that empirical data would leave the subset of societies displaying perfect equality a very empty set indeed.

ciety as a whole, there also exists a potential increase in the wealth of the poorer segments of the society. By utilizing the political realm where the rules of the game are made, the poorest half of society plus one could theoretically impose extensive taxes upon the wealth and incomes of those at the top and give themselves transfer payments which could increase both their real income and wealth positions.

It might be argued that this would in some way violate the constitutional rules established in most democratic societies, but given enough votes these rules can alway be modified without limit. If the mass does not exercise its potential strength there must be a reason. In our system the mass has both the motivation in terms of real income, and the means in the form of votes to eliminate the privileged position of the elite. It was perhaps a fear of just such an occurrence which led the framers of the democratic structure in the United States originally to limit the vote to land-holding males. Yet with the legal extensions of suffrage to new elements of society we still do not witness real equalization of incomes and wealth.[8] Why is this so? Are the majority of voters irrational in the sense that they refuse to take advantage of a potential increase in their relative wealth positions? Are political parties irrational to the extent that they never seem to propose effective policies of widespread equalization, even though they ostensibly should appeal to a majority of the voters? Clearly, we must either abandon our assumption of rationality, or we must provide some explanation for this type of behavior which does not contradict the assumption.

Two possible explanations of this nature come to mind, both of which rely rather heavily upon the system of political decision making through the subsidization of information acquisition and resource trading which was the foundation of the earlier portions of the book. The first explanation stems from the presence of a widespread system of

---

[8] Note that in certain areas and situations the *de jure* extension of suffrage has not always been accompanied by *de facto* extension. Extra-legal or illegal means may be used to deny the implementation of changes in voting criteria. Even with federal rulings guaranteeing voting rights, significant elements of the black southern population are effectively disenfranchised. The firmness with which old patterns are maintained may in part be explained by a fear that massive black voting will reduce the elite status of whites, who are often in a minority. It is precisely a fear that the political arena will be used to redistribute values away from the elite that leads it to restrict the use of voting power to those who accept the status quo.

thought, a collection of moral precepts in the form of an ideology, which explains and justifies the current distribution of values in the society. It often ties the future welfare of the system and its members to the maintenance of this distribution. All societies have such an ideology; the actual precepts differ, but the presence of an ideology is universal. There may or may not be significant normative differences in the precepts of different ideologies. One may be better than others. A ranking of ideologies is a problem for moral philosophers; our problem requires only that an ideology exist and that it be widely believed. It need be no better or no worse than alternatives. Then to the extent that the mass *believes* that the welfare of society and hence their own welfare depends upon the structure of society as explained by the dominant ideology, their acceptance of inequality in the distribution of values is rational.

Alternatively, we might be able to provide an explanation for long-term inequality revolving around the information individual consumers have as to the distribution of values, their place within it, and the net gain they may expect to receive from equalization. This explanation seems less plausible when taken in isolation, but it may be combined with the ideological one to provide a strong picture of rational behavior over the long term.

We have seen that short term tax-expenditure decisions will reflect the distributions of wealth and resources which in turn distinguish the elite from the mass. Inequality in the distribution will be reflected in the outcome of these decisions. The mass has both the ability and the motivation to reduce this inequality in wealth and decision making but the ability goes largely unused. By examining these two explanations of long-term behavior in the next few pages, we may be able to come to an understanding of why.

CHAPTER 17
THE ROLE
OF IDEOLOGY

The rich man in his castle
The poor man at his gate
God made them high and lowly
And ordered their estate

Traditional Hymn

Whether or not ideology can be eliminated from the world of thought in the social sciences, it is certainly indispensible in the world of action in social life. A society cannot exist unless its members have common feelings about what is the proper way of conducting its affairs, and these common feelings are expressed in ideology.

Joan Robinson

Any economic system requires a set of rules, an ideology to justify them, and a conscience in the individual which makes him strive to carry them out.

Joan Robinson

We can observe systems of belief in all societies. Groups of men who tend to identify themselves as distinct groups have certain perceptions of the world in common. Often it is the sharing of these perceptions which defines the membership of the group. These common thoughts and values can be systematically interwoven to form an ideology, the common doctrines of a people. The presence of ideologies is a universally accepted phenomenon among social scientists. Few indeed would question their existence, but the role they play and their importance in forming the structure of societies is an area of disagreement. Let us begin by presenting one of the more limited, short-run views of the ideological role, and then turn to longer range views which fit more closely with the problem at hand.

One view of the role of ideology has been expressed by Anthony Downs. In his *Economic Theory of Democracy*, he stresses the important role of party, as opposed to national, ideologies in the determination of voting patterns.[1] Due to the uncertainty voters face with

---

[1] Anthony Downs, *op. cit.*, especially Chapters 7 and 8.

regard to the policy positions taken by different parties over the entire range of possible issues, and due to the costs and difficulty of overcoming this uncertainty, Downs claims that it may be rational for voters to reach voting decisions on the basis of ideologies rather than issues. Each voter can compare the ideology of the party with his own personal philosophy more easily than he can compare the party's policy positions with his own. This stems from the fact that there are fewer basic ideological premises than there are possible policy positions. Moreover, the ideology of a party will supposedly remain relatively stable over time and hence reduce the need for investments in much new information each election period.

> Uncertainty restricts each voter's ability to relate every governmental act to his own view of the good society. Therefore, acquaintance with each party's view of the good society—its ideology—helps him make his voting decision without knowing about every policy specifically. Voters thus use ideologies to cut their information costs.[2]

Without question, if voters place confidence in the pronouncements of political parties, and if they are indeed trying to minimize their costs of reaching an informed voting decision, then the use of party ideologies as an inexpensive means of distinguishing between opposing parties is rational. However, this is a precept which is based strictly on the short run in terms of time dimensions, and on the marginal, as opposed to central, differences in ideology. If we are truly to come to an understanding of the nature of political society under democratic governmental forms we must examine this problem from a broader viewpoint, i.e., in long-run, central terms.

The comparison of party ideologies with personal philosophies is an act which occurs relatively late in the process of forming political and ideological preferences. In Chapter 3 we discussed the formation of preference functions with the possibility of external influence. This same process of influence is used in all societies to impose upon its members the basic precepts of national, as opposed to party, ideology. Societies, in part, form the values of their members. "The content of conscience, like the particular language that is learned, depends upon the society in which the individual grows up."[3]

---

[2] *Ibid.*, p. 113.
[3] Joan Robinson, *Economic Philosophy*, Doubleday and Co., Garden City, New York, Anchor Books edition, 1964, p. 7.

Anthropologists call the process "acculturation," others call it "indoctrination," still others "education"; by any name, there exists a process by which any social organization attempts to perpetuate itself by instilling and reinforcing its basic philosophy in the minds of its members. To speak of comparing party ideologies with personal philosophy is to begin analysis after this process has taken place, and moreover, this process has economic aspects and political effects which must be considered in any long range view of society.

> Any well-knit way of life molds human behavior in its own design. The individualism of bourgeois society like the communism of a socialized state must be inculcated from the nursery to the grave. In the United States, as one among the bourgeois nations, the life of personal achievement and personal responsibility is extolled in song and story from the very beginning of consciousness. Pennybanks instill the habit of thrift; trading in the schoolyard propagates the bourgeois scale of values. . . .
>
> When such an ideology impregnates life from start to finish, the thesis of collective responsibility runs against a wall of non-comprehension. In any collective society, the texture of life experience would need to be respun.[4]

Party ideologies generally propose marginal variations in the operation of the system. They neither oppose, nor offer significant possible alterations in the national ideology. It is an umbrella which covers all the marginal differences of major parties in a stable political state. For example, the national ideology of the United States relies on a belief in the responsibility of an individual for his own situation and in the sanctity of private ownership and control of the means of production. Free markets are national shrines. No major political party could seriously propose the nationalization of all industry and the introduction of centralized planning to supersede the market and still hope to be elected. In Downs' terms the party ideology would diverge from the personal philosophy of a majority of the voters. In our terms the national ideology in part created this personal philosophy. Such policies and the ideologies represented by them violate the basic tenets of the national ideology. The type of differences observed in party ideologies, such as disagreement over the desirability of taxing business rather than persons, do not violate these basic doctrines.

We must begin our analysis of political and economic effects on the long term structure of society by examining this *national* ideol-

----

4 Lasswell, *op. cit.*, pp. 32–34.

ogy rather than party ideologies. There are two central aspects of national ideologies which must be made explicitly clear in such an analysis. First, they provide a system of thought which justifies the distribution of values within the society—whether it be democratic, totalitarian or socialist—and secondly, these ideologies do not arise simultaneously, yet independently, in all the members of a state. They are both explicitly learned and consciously taught.

IDEOLOGICAL JUSTIFICATION OF VALUE DISTRIBUTION

The basic precepts of any national ideology tend to provide philosophical explanations of the discrepancies in value endowments which the mass may observe. For example, the strong emphasis upon individual responsibility and equality of opportunity in American society creates a belief that the relative positions of different individuals depend upon their efforts. Hard work merits and will receive large rewards; a lack of productivity brings with it well-deserved poverty. Individuals are paid according to the amount they contribute to the production of real goods and services and hence those with the highest rewards are regarded as having contributed the most whether this is objectively verifiable or not. It is regarded as "un-American" to suggest depriving a man of the fruits of his labors, particularly if they are to be shared with "less productive" individuals. The question here is not one of the value of these precepts in terms of some absolute standards of "good" and "bad," or even one of their validity. What is important here is that they are widely held and strongly believed, and that they do provide a justification for the inequality in the distribution of values.

This aspect of ideologies is a universal in the Lasswellian framework. All societies have a set of values justifying what is. It is easy to see these aspects of ideologies in "opposing" societies even if it is less obvious in the case of one's own. The organic view of society which is typical of fascist states such as Nazi Germany is built around the concept that individuals act as cells in the body of the total state. They perform specialized functions which benefit the whole rather than themselves. In this type of value system equality is of little importance since the welfare of the individual derives directly from the welfare of the whole. As long as the state in its entirety is enjoying the maximum possible vitality, the individual should be satisfied. To the extent that this ideology is believed, it provides a justification for the inequality in the distribution of values and will lead the mass to accept, and perhaps even defend it. Again, it matters not whether this view of society is correct, or even if there is any such thing as "correct" with regard to ideologies; all that matters is that it be believed.

The ideology of a truly communistic state also serves this same purpose of providing justification. "From each according to his ability; to each according to his need." To the extent that people believe this principle and the fact that needs may differ, they will accept and defend inequality in the distribution of values. Since, in practice, the determination of "needs" would probably be made by the elite, we might expect them to weight their own relatively heavily.

Justification of the status quo by national ideologies is by no means a new development in human society. It is probably most easily seen and accepted in the historical past, perhaps because we have not been exposed to any "acculturation" of now obsolete ideologies. For centuries, monarchs ruled with absolute power in both the east and the west under the banner of the "divine right of kings." Having been granted wealth and power by God himself, monarchs could regard challenges to their privilege as both treasonably and sacrilegious. To the extent that the mass *believed* this justification of the situation, it was satisfied that the distribution of values was both inevitable and just.

A further point has been suggested here and its importance is great—the *elite* will often believe and defend the ideology just as strongly as the mass. It is seldom an act of conscious deception when the elite stresses the sanctity of the national ideology. It is accepted and believed by them as well. As members of a society they learn to adhere to its basic philosophy as a matter of course, just as does the mass.

> The ethical system implanted in each of us by our upbringing (even a rebel is influenced by what he rebels against) was not derived from any reasonable principles; those who conveyed it to us were rarely able to give any rational account of it, or indeed to formulate it explicitly at all. They handed on to us what society had taught them, in the same way as they handed on to us the language they had learned to speak.[5]

If it is deception to use ideological principles, it must be regarded as an act of self-deception, or rather universal and mutual deception of the entire society by itself. It is seldom a conspiracy of oppression.

[5] Joan Robinson, *op. cit.*, p. 12.

Ideologies are present in nearly all members of a society, however, and given our emphasis on externally generated influence in the earlier pages of this book it should not come as a surprise that we claim that the widespread existence of these ideologies is not totally accidental. Nor is the extent of their acceptance dependent upon a vast number of individuals independently reaching similar philosophical conclusions in the absence of influence. Ideologies are learned by all members of a society, whether mass or elite; they are therefore also taught.

THE IMPOSITION OF IDEOLOGY

The central ideas of any society are instilled in its members through an extensive program of acculturation. This takes place in societies which have known ideological stability for years, but it also takes place, and is more obvious, in societies which have experienced a recent change in elites necessitating an alteration of the national ideology. A commonly noted characteristic of post-revolutionary governments is a program of "re-educating" the people and of suppressing "counter-revolutionary" thought. This often involves a degree of coercion in the sense that people may suffer real punishments for rejecting the new "truth" while they are often rewarded for openly accepting it. It also includes alterations in the relative prices of different bits of information with respect to the pre-revolutionary ratios. The good points of the new elite are stressed, along with the reasons for the revolution; the evils of the old and its injustices are often mentioned. This information will be provided at a subsidized rate to the entire society. Such a process is often condemned as a form of thought control, and indeed it is that, but it is by no means limited to revolutionary governments and societies. It is merely most obvious there.

A further example of the explicit manipulation of national ideologies to justify a new elite may be seen in Nazi Germany. Hitler's vast campaigns of propaganda, his organization of the "Hitler Youth," his emphasis on Naziism in the curriculum of German schools, and his massive rallies and insistence upon an organic view of the state and its mission were all attempts to affect the perceptions of the German mass and hence its ideology. These all involved alteration of the relative prices of information, partly through subsidization, and partly by raising the price of acquiring unfavorable information with the threat of violence. To a rather significant degree he was successful in his attempts.

In well-established societies, enjoying ideological stability, this process of acculturation still occurs, but it takes less obvious forms and requires less coercion and also less expenditure of resources by the elite.

> An ideology, once accepted, perpetuates itself with remarkable vitality. The individuals born into the state direct some of their love toward the symbols which sustain the system: the common name, the common heroes, the common mission, the common demands. Some destructive tendencies are directed against rivals, traitors, heresies and counter-demands.[6]

As soon as one generation comes to accept the ideology, then the task of instilling it in the next passes out of the hands of the elite and becomes an automatic activity of the mass itself. Parents teach their children to accept certain concepts as true and good, others as false and evil. Schools spend a great deal of time and effort educating children about the requirements and responsibilities of good citizenship. They teach that the existing society is the best of all possible ones. They teach children to revere the symbols of the ideology and its catchwords—whether these be the American flag or the swastika, the Pledge of Allegiance or the Communist Manifesto, George Washington or Mao Tse-tung. It is not coincidental that American children tend to regard Lenin as evil and Russian children to regard him as good. They are both taught to do so.

Moreover, the entire culture of the society will come to reflect and glorify the ideological principles without any conscious guidance by the elite. In the United States

> Gossip, fiction, motion pictures sustain the thesis of personal responsibility for failure or success. He failed because he lacked tact or had halitosis or didn't finish his education. . . . She was successful because she got the right shade of lipstick, took French lessons at home on the phonograph, kept the skin you love to touch. . . . In "I'm No Angel" the ex-carnival girl marries a society man. In "Morning Glory" a stage-struck country girl is shoved into the star part on the opening night of a play and makes a hit. . . .

while in the Soviet Union

> Group tasks supplant individual tasks in order to keep collective enterprises rather than ambitious persons at the center of attention. Theatricals emphasize the play and not the star, and treat the fate of movements rather than the problems of the individual person.[7]

[6] Lasswell, *op. cit.,* p. 169.
[7] *Ibid.,* pp. 33–34.

In all societies there is an ideology which arises and is perpetuated either through a conscious program directed by an elite, or through the automatic process of acculturating each new generation to the dominant beliefs of its society. Whether one ideology is better than another in some absolute sense is a value judgment we are unqualified to make. We claim only that each society has an ideology which provides a justification for the status quo, and that it is a learned ideology. In a book such as this we wish to examine the economic aspects of this learning process in the context of the rational behavior of self-interested agents. We turn now to that less volatile question.

CHAPTER 18

RATIONAL RESPONSE TO IDEOLOGY

A sucker is born every minute.

P. T. Barnum

The individual human organism at birth is essentially an ideological and factual blank. On the basis of his experiences and the information he acquires from other humans regarding their experiences and knowledge he begins to form his own view of the world. Different inputs into this process will result in different philosophical and ideological outputs. Children, if they are rational, will accept as inputs into the formation of their personalities and ideologies those informational items which are offered at the lowest cost. Few American children have the desire or the ability to travel to the Soviet Union or China to be told what values are important in society. If they are trying to minimize the costs and discomfort of learning (and what child isn't) they will be content to acquire that information from their parents since it is available at a much lower relative price.

Similarly, since the experience of children is inevitably limited they will be unable to form an effective discount to be applied to the information received from their home culture. However, one aspect of the home culture is the formation of discount factors which are applied to foreign ideologies. It is rational to assimilate the domestic ideology and rational to be unaware of, or reject, opposing ideologies strictly on the basis of cost minimization.

As children mature and become adults they must continue to formulate and re-evaluate their particular ideology on the basis of past experience, the information they have accumulated in this way in the past, and upon newly acquired information. As in all previous cases of decision making in the face of uncertainty, information will be acquired according to the relative costs of various items, though certain sources of information may call into play a discount factor which lowers the perceived value of information from that source. The dominant ideology will be perpetuated, or a new one will replace it, on the basis of the relative price schedules for informational items and the scale of discount factors. The control of information and the ability to influence the prices of various items carries with it the ability to influence ideological belief. This is particularly true since information in this type of process can and will include not only facts (if such exist) but also interpretations of facts and systems of thought for analyzing them.

For example, each society has a particular view of history that it teaches to each succeeding generation. History is never totally objective, however, for it is always recorded from the point of view of an observer. People studying the record of history are presented explicitly with a sequence of events and either implicitly or explicitly with this particular point of view. American students of the Russian revolution are presented with low cost facts as to the casualties caused by the Bolsheviks in their bloody "purges" and with explanations of the failure of the revolution from the capitalistic point of view. Russian students are presented with low cost facts as to the corruption of the Czar, his oppression of the masses, and the necessity and success of the revolution from the socialist viewpoint. To either group, the costs of understanding the opposite interpretation are substantially raised since it requires direct research outside of the normal process of education, utilizing sources to which a significant discount factor is normally affixed.

Similarly, Americans are presented with low cost information as to the necessity of American intervention in Southeast Asia for the preservation of freedom and the containment of communistic slavery. People in the Socialist countries receive subsidized information stressing the role of the United States in crushing the freedom of already oppressed peoples in order to protect American investments and profits. Facts carry not only objective information, but they are generally accompanied by interpretations and explanations of phenomena. The relative prices of these interpretations as well as of information itself will influence the acquisitions of individuals. Rational cost minimization will lead to a bias in the acceptance of information toward the low-cost, subsidized items.

There are also aspects of rational behavior on the part of an elite group responding to the presence of, or need for, a national ideology. These can be examined in the context of two distinctly different situations; first, the replacement of one ideology by another and, secondly, the maintenance of an accepted ideology over time. Both of these situations can be analyzed from the point of view of economic responses to information prices. In the process of analysis we will also be able to provide explanations for certain observed phenomena as the results of the rational pursuit of economic goals.

IDEOLOGICAL REPLACEMENT

Rapid changes in the structure of the elite take place following any revolution. In order for the revolution to be successful in the first place it is necessary for there to be significant numbers of individuals who have rejected the established ideology in favor of another. Yet the entire populace will not have done so, for if they had, violent revolution would not have been necessary. Hence, following the overthrow of one elite by another the problem of the ideological orientation of the society will be great. A justification for the new order must come into acceptance. Yet the mass will have been sufficiently supplied with low-cost information as to the desirability of the previous ideology that it will not be easily susceptible to changes in that ideology. Their political preferences will have been already formed. As a result, large scale programs of conscious "re-education" are required that would not be necessary with an established ideology. We generally see extreme alterations in the relative prices of favorable and unfavorable information (including the interpretation of facts). This often takes the form of charging a very high price for *not* acquiring favorable information. If the new elite imposes financial or corporal penalties on those individuals who either continue to accept the old ideology or refuse to claim allegiance to the new one, the price of obtaining unfavorable information becomes excessive. A member of the mass who knows that the reading of certain material could result in loss of freedom, loss of property, or even loss of life must think twice before doing so. If he knows that similar punishments may come from *not* acquiring new favorable information, he will be inclined to acquire it. He will respond to price incentives, even if they are not presented in pure money terms.

We could expect to see a two-part strategy undertaken by revolutionary governments in response to this characteristic of rational agents. The use of purely economic pricing of information in the face of widespread resistance will be prohibitively expensive; hence the government will provide large amounts of "free" information consisting of favorable facts and interpretations, and also will use coercion to lower the *relative* price of this information below its economic level. Similarly, coercion will be used to raise the costs of acquiring unfavorable information.

The optimal strategy for the government and the new elite to follow will vary among different subgroups of the mass. Different aspects of ideological alteration will be more effective when concentrated on different segments of society, and this effectiveness will arise from economic considerations.

In Chapter 2 we showed that the presence of a large discount factor effectively raises the amount of favorable information required to cause an alteration in an individual's decisions with regard to an issue. We have also seen that the presentation of "free" or subsidized information is really only costless from the point of view of the recipient. The producer and distributor of this subsidized information incurs real costs in the form of resource expenditures whenever he presents it to the recipients. The greater the amount of information provided at reduced price, the greater the costs incurred by the producer. In the case of altering an existing ideology the producer is the new elite, the recipient is the mass.

Hence, the greater the discount factor which the mass, or portions of it, apply to the new information provided by the incoming elite, the more expensive it will be for the elite to alter the ideological beliefs of the mass. Similarly, the more firmly instilled is the old ideology, the greater will be the value of this discount factor.

Adult populations, for the most part, have been subjected to large quantities of information and interpretation provided by the previous elite. They have been fully acculturated. One of the significant aspects of this acculturation is the imposition of a large discount factor to be applied to information presented by "opposing" elites, whether internal or external to the state in question. To fully overcome this discount factor would be extremely expensive. It would be less expensive to require verbal allegiance to the new ideology by using coercion than actually to cause the adult population to internalize it.

Children, however, have not been fully acculturated to the old beliefs and do not, therefore, possess such great discount factors with regard to new information. They are thus more susceptible to attempts at causing internalization of the new ideology at an acceptable cost. They can be brought to complete acceptance and defense of the new system of thought at a lower cost per individual than can the adult population.

As a result of this situation, and of a desire on the part of the new elite to minimize the costs of maintaining dominance, we witness a concentration on the education of the young into the new ideology, coupled with coercive controls to prevent interference with this by the older generation. In some cases this may take the extreme form of separating children from "questionable" parents, or even of turning them into agents of control over them. The importance of the Hitler Youth in the establishment of Naziism and the cases where members turned in their parents for rejection of the party philosophy are representative of such a strategy. Similarly, the citizenship training of students in post-revolutionary schools often exhibits this approach. In fact, some of the "Freedom Schools" in the black ghettoes of the U.S. demonstrate attempts at altering ideological perceptions at a young age when resistance and hence costs are lowest.

If the elite is trying to minimize its costs of coming to power, and if the imposition of a new ideology requires expenditures for both coercion (rule by force) and for re-education (rule by information), why then doesn't the new elite rely solely upon force and eliminate the costs of re-education? While such a policy might be desirable over the short run, it is the long-run stream of costs which is of the greatest importance. As we have seen, a well-established ideology allows an elite to maintain its privileged position almost without cost to itself; an indoctrinated mass assumes the responsibility for acculturating the next generation and perpetuating the ideology. A mass ruled by force alone requires a continuous and conscious effort on the part of the elite to insure its dominance. Such an effort entails excessive use of resources and time in each time period. There is a real limit to the use of these resource stocks over time if the mass is ruled by ideology; at some point the costs diminish significantly.

Given anything longer than a very brief time horizon, the stream of costs required to maintain dominance through force will exceed that of maintaining it through ideological imposition. In the very short run this may not be so, but in the long run it will. Before we continue in this line of argument, let us turn to a brief digression concerning the nature of elites which will relate the discussion above more clearly to our main concern, democratically organized political systems. The question may be raised as to why a government which faces potential removal within a short-time horizon should concern itself with long-run cost streams. Its power position may not extend beyond the next election date. While this question might be partially answered by claiming that governments wish to assure re-election, thus expanding their time horizon, and that over this extended horizon they need to utilize resources to influence voters' utility rather than to enforce dominance, such an answer would not be completely adequate. We could, instead, arrive at a better answer by looking at the concept of the elite as it was first defined relative to the concept of government. The two are *not* identical. In our system we distinguish between a formal elite (a visible elite, the government) and an informal (less visible, less institutionalized) elite. In such a system the informal elite is more permanent since it is not subject to the periodic formal ratification of its position by the mass. It has a disproportionate share of the values and as a result has the greatest ability to influence the policy decisions of the formal elite. There may be cross-membership between the two groups and individuals may pass from one to the other and back.[1] It is this informal elite which is at the top of the scale of the distribution of values, and it is they who enjoy the long term permanency which entails a need to consider long term cost streams. Their time horizon is not bounded by the length of the election period.

The changes in government which occur within democratic societies are not representative of a change in elites—they represent a continuation of the same informal elite and the maintenance of the existing ideology. Only when a democratic form of government replaces a nondemocratic one (or vice versa) will there be a change of elites requiring the utilization of those strategies outlined above. In those cases the new elite would have to engage in a program of ideological imposition with regard to the new system of thought.

Having clarified that point, let us return to the original problem, the economic aspects of ideological imposition. We have discussed them already in the case of altering the nature of the national ideology. Yet this is not sufficient as an explanation of all situations. There are also economic aspects of maintaining an already established ideology.

IDEOLOGICAL PERPETUATION

We have already discussed in some detail the fact that the costs to the elite of maintaining an ideology, once it has been accepted by the

---

[1] Such interlocking of membership in the formal and informal circles of power is a central theme in C. Wright Mills, *The Power Elite, op. cit.*

mass, are quite low. The existence of a large amount of information in the hands of the mass, along with a favorable interpretation of the facts, automatically lowers the price of this information to new generations. Acculturation still results from the reaction to the relative prices of favorable and unfavorable information but this pricing no longer requires any conscious, explicit activity on the part of the elite.[2]

One aspect central to ideologies is an innate distrust of information which is favorable to opposing ideologies. This is a characteristic which is passed along in the process of acculturation and hence is independent of activity on the part of the elite. Its existence serves as an economic protection of the elite, however, because it raises the cost to any counter-elite of assuming power. There are two distinct aspects of this phenomenon.

First, there is the other side of the problem discussed under the section on the alteration of ideologies. To the extent that the cost of altering the previously established ideology following a revolution is increased, it may act as a deterrent to revolution. If the counter-elite feels it will be unable to maintain control after the revolution, then such action becomes unfeasible. To be sure, this depends upon the counter-elite's *estimations* of future costs which in turn depend upon information, but the effect certainly exists.

The second aspect of discount factors is that they tend to prohibit the alteration of the elite through legal means, as opposed to revolution, since such action becomes prohibitively expensive. A large discount factor applied by the mass to information from counter-elites raises the total amount and hence the total cost of enough subsidized information to cause acceptance of the new ideology. If the discount factor becomes infinite, there is no possibility of meeting the costs. The amount of information provided to American citizens by, say, the Soviet Union's elite necessary to make them reject U.S. capitalism in favor of Russian socialism is immense and perhaps infinite—such information can be discounted as part of a "communist conspiracy" and is not to be believed. The amount of information broadcast over Radio Free Europe necessary to cause the Russian people to reject socialism in favor of Western capitalism is similarly large—it is an "imperialist

---

[2] It seems prudent once again to stress the fact that the ideology being imposed is probably firmly believed by the elite as well as the mass. This is not really surprising since it is the elite who benefits most from the system of thought. They may be expected to believe that that view of the world is truly best which is also best for them.

trick." This tendency is further reinforced by the ability of the established elite in the state to use coercion to alter the relative price of this free information. As long as the counter-elite lacks the ability to use force necessary to alter the price and availability of information sufficiently, the high discount factor which accompanies an established ideology serves to protect the position of the established elite.

The efficient alteration of an established ideology requires the use of coercion as well as information pricing as we have seen, and it is for this reason that we observe most major alterations in the informal elite by revolution. There can and does occur an alteration in the formal elite each election period under democratic organization but the imposition of socialism in a democracy would probably require revolution. Republicans can replace Democrats in office without using the power of force—communists realistically cannot since this would entail the reformulation of the informal elite as well. Members of the Soviet formal elite may jockey for power positions without resorting to widespread violence—a capitalist or a democrat does not have the same options. Established ideologies protect the position of the informal elite by raising the costs of their removal to a level requiring, in most cases, armed revolution.[3]

ACCEPTANCE OF IDEOLOGIES BY MASSES

It is apparent that the use of ideologies to promote dominance is a cost minimizing strategy for the elite. The question may then arise as to why the mass, which is certainly less benefited by the imposition of the ideology than the elite, should actually accept it. Once again the answer can be found in strategies of rational cost minimization.

We can be certain that the individuals who make up the mass are, like all agents in our system, subject to a high degree of uncertainty. They must make their market and political decisions on the basis of imperfect information. In order to avoid the costs of incorrect decisions, they will invest time and resources in the acquisition of a certain amount of information in an attempt to improve the probability of reaching correct decisions. Information is not without cost, however, and there is thus a limit to the amount that can be acquired. More-

[3] Let us emphasize once again our intention to avoid value judgments. Revolutions *per se* are neither good nor bad. They do not represent the elimination of elites in any case—they consist only of an alteration in the class composition of the elite.

over, we have assumed a goal of utility maximization for individuals, and since each expenditure for information reduces the amount left over for the purchase of other utility producing goods, the amount it is rational to acquire will be quite limited. As always, the composition of this stock of information will depend upon the various relative prices of different items, and to the extent that the elite can control these prices they can affect the information upon which decisions are based. Rational members of the mass will acquire the low-cost information which results in acculturation of the established ideology, or in the case of changes in elites of the new ideology.

The rationality of this behavior of acceptance can be seen even more clearly in the case of a single member who, for some exogenous reason, begins to doubt the validity of the established ideology. The costs to him of acquiring information detrimental to the elite are, as we have seen, relatively high. Yet assuming he were willing to incur these, and that having done so he rejected the established ideology, he would still be faced with more costs before his rejection would matter to the elite. Personal rejection of an ideology has a negligible effect on the functioning of a system. It is only when significantly large numbers of individuals reject the ideology that material changes can be expected. Therefore, our individual must also incur the costs of subsidizing the acquisition of information by other members of the mass in an effort to recruit sufficient numbers to his position. This will be harder to do as the size of the discount factor applied by the rest of the mass increases. Finally, there are then the costs of organizing the newly recruited agents into a group able to act, and these costs can be, and often are, substantially raised by the threatened but still powerful elite. The costs to those members of the Russian intelligentsia who publicly criticize the state rather exceed the costs of acquiring information. The costs to the Black Panthers and other radical groups of rejecting the dominant ideology of the United States and acting upon that rejection have similarly been raised. Coercion as well as the costs of information will lead to the rational acceptance of the ideology of the established state.

Any individual examining this situation *ex ante* will be faced with extremely high expected costs and very small expected gain from the effort involved in personally rejecting and then attempting to alter the current ideology. It is far less costly for the mass to acquire the low-cost information provided by the elite and the acculturated mass than to incur the costs of rejecting it. Any individual member of the mass is made better off by following such a strategy; the mass is the sum of these individual members.

"FRINGE BENEFITS" OF IDEOLOGIES

In addition to allowing long run inequality in the distribution of values within a society, an ideology also provides a method of cost minimization with regard to short term decisions, as seen by both the decider and those who may wish to influence the decision. There are certain symbols associated with an ideology which take on high importance and lend credence and desirability to any position which can be associated with them. "By the use of sanctioned words and gestures the elite elicits blood, work, taxes, applause from the masses."[4] It is far cheaper to influence the actions of the mass by appealing to "patriotic duty" and "national tradition" than it is to provide extensive amounts of subsidized information as to the "objective" advisibility of those actions. Once an ideology has been accepted, its symbols and precepts provide low-cost methods of influencing short-run decisions on particular issues.

There are also benefits for the mass, or other deciders as well, in terms of cost minimization with regard to particular issues. These fall closely in line with Downs' analysis of ideologies' role in voting decisions. He claimed that voters could compare their personal philosophies with party ideologies and vote on that basis without having to compare a vast number of policy positions. This same idea can be applied to non-voting decisions as well. Once it has accepted an ideology, it is far cheaper for the mass to decide on actions in support of policies on the basis of appeals to this "patriotic duty" than on the basis of analyzing much larger amounts of factual information even if it is provided at a subsidized rate. Ideologies reduce the costs faced by influencer and influenced once they have been accepted as the correct view of the world.

Masses can thus be called forth to action by the mere use of symbols in a sort of conditioned response. American soldiers fight wars in the defense of "apple pie and motherhood" but in the entire scope of human history there had never been a war fought over anything as mundane as an apple pie. Not even Ho Chi Minh represented any

---

[4] Lasswell, *op. cit.*, p. 31.

significant threat to American apple pies. Wars are fought over conflicts of power as elites and countries try to re-allocate the international distribution of values. But it is cheaper to recruit soldiers on the basis of glory and apple pie than it is on the basis of creating a belief in the desirability of altering an elite's international position. This is of course most apparent in the case of offensive as opposed to defensive wars, since in this case it is most obviously the elite which benefits while it is the mass which bears the burden of the actual fighting.

CONCLUSIONS

An ideology is a system of thought underlying a society which justifies the rules by which that society operates and hence also justifies the outcome of that operation. It provides a rationale for the status quo and its perpetuation. Some ideologies may be better than others; or they may not. They are based upon normative precepts which cannot be judged in a truly objective treatise. The choice among ideologies must be a problem for philosophers. What is important at this point is that they all provide an explanation for the distribution of values which, in the real world, implies an explanation of a greater or lesser degree of inequality in the distribution. To the extent that the ideology is believed, it can assure the long-term continuation of the inequality.

Certain characteristics of national ideologies are apparent, and their presence and imposition represent economic behavior on the part of both the mass and the elite.

1. An ideology is the cheapest way of insuring the dominance of the elite over the long run. This is particularly true since the acculturation of new generations is essentially costless to the elite once the ideology has been accepted. The costs of enforcing dominance by coercion are substantially higher.
2. A change in the elites in a society requires an alteration of the national ideology. The costs of alteration can be minimized by following a two-part strategy of using force to magnify the relative price of unfavorable information and using subsidization to provide vast amounts of low cost, favorable information.
3. These costs can also be reduced by concentrating the coercion on the older members of the society who have a high discount factor for new information, while at the same time concentrating the

new information most heavily on those members of the mass with the lowest discounts, i.e., the children.

4. The acceptance of the ideology by both the mass and the elite is the end result of rational attempts to reduce uncertainty as to the nature of the world at a minimal cost.

5. An accepted ideology serves to raise the costs to a counter-elite of gaining power, since it normally makes the amount of new information necessary to change the ideology peacefully so large that it becomes prohibitively expensive. This stems from the fact that ideologies include discount factors which lower the effectiveness of information detrimental to the established order and patterns of thought.

6. There are symbols associated with any ideology which allow for the low-cost manipulation of short-term actions of the mass by reducing the need for providing large quantities of information at subsidized costs on each issue.

7. Ideological influence, like all other influence, depends to a large degree on the ability of one group to control the relative prices of favorable and unfavorable information for other groups. Whenever the costs of producing influence are less than the expected gain, our postulate of rationality in the pursuit of self-interest requires it to be undertaken.

CHAPTER 19
INFORMATIONAL
EXPLANATION

It is true that you may fool all the people some of the time; you may even fool some of the people all of the time; but you can't fool all of the people all of the time.

Abraham Lincoln

When we first posed the question of the absence of equality in the distribution of values, we claimed that such a situation could occur in a democracy only if the majority of the voters believed it was justified, or alternatively, if they were unaware of its existence. We have just outlined in some depth the nature of the first condition. It is now necessary to look at the informational case where voters are ignorant of the exact nature of the distribution of values or of their actual position in it, or both. It will become apparent that under the postulated motivations of the groups in our system this type of explanation is really only adequate in discussing the short run. It will not completely explain the continued existence of inequality over a longer period.

If voters are truly utility maximizers, and if the greater their real incomes, the greater their ability to gain utility, they will be susceptible to any proposed policy which promises to raise the real incomes of a majority of them. If a majority of the voters could gain by a reduction in the incomes of the very rich, then in a world of perfect certainty they will vote to do so. Moreover, in such a world any party desiring to be elected would have to advocate such a policy since it would lead to direct increases in the utility of a majority of the voters, and they would be aware of parties' behavior which left these increases unrealized. From the point of view of office seeking politicians, to ignore these potential increases would be to invite defeat.

Ours is not a world of perfect certainty, however, and perhaps the degree of awareness on the part of the voters is not so great as to cause them to openly clamor for equality, even assuming for a moment a lack of ideological justification for inequality. We would then not expect to see each party advocating equality with any degree of vehemence, at least in any given election campaign.

However, we have postulated vote maximization as the primary motivating force behind political parties' behavior, and as a result we would expect to see some party provide voters with subsidized information as to the nature of the distribution of values in the society in an attempt to increase its relative vote position. This information would also include facts as to the positions of different classes of voters within the overall distribution and the gains each group could expect from the proposed equalization policies. Assuming the rational pursuit of utility on the part of voters, such a program should lead to an acquisition of a majority of the votes by the party proposing it, as soon as a sufficient number of voters have acquired a sufficient amount of information. At this point equalization would become inevitable since all parties desiring office would have to advocate such a policy, and any party elected must carry it out or be faced with removal from office in the next election.

The long-term maintenance of inequality in the distribution of values could only occur under one of several peculiar sets of circumstances. In the absence of these conditions, and under the behavioral postulates of our democratic, market system inequality could not be long maintained.

PARTY IGNORANCE

If all political parties suffer from a high degree of uncertainty as to the nature of the distribution of values, they will be unable to provide information to the voters. If they are all uncertain as to the desires of voters to increase their real incomes at the expense of others, they may not utilize what information they have. However, as soon as one party overcomes this uncertainty, all parties must adopt equalization policies.

VOTER DISCOUNTING OF INFORMATION

The amount of information necessary to inform voters of the nature of the distribution of values and their expected benefits from equalization depends directly on the size of the discount factor voters hold for such information. If this discount factor is extremely large, the stock of information necessary to affect behavior may be prohibitively large. (Note that the most probable cause of a high discount factor is the presence of an established ideology which justifies the distribution in the minds of most voters.) If such a discount exists, parties may find it economical to refrain from exploiting the issue due to the high costs of providing sufficient amounts of subsidized information.

CAMPAIGNS OF "OPPOSING" INFORMATION

If voters are simultaneously presented with a variety of influence-producing campaigns consisting of programs of subsidized information which lead to conflicting conclusions, the end result in terms of voting behavior is indeterminate. If those agents on the top of the value distribution (those who stand to lose the most under equalization) provide voters with information equating the rights of middle and lower groups to enjoy moderate wealth with their own rights to enjoy more extreme wealth, it is no longer clear that a party will realize a net gain by proposing equalization. To the extent that voters are convinced by the informational campaigns of the top level agents, they will regard parties advocating equalization as potentially detrimental to their achievement of maximum utility. Under these circumstances, or the threat of them, parties may not be willing to incur the risks of attempting to exploit the issue of inequality. (These risks will obviously be more pronounced if there exists an ideology, the symbols of which may be called forth by the top groups at very low cost to protect their position. Ideologies will reduce the costs of counter-influence by those groups enjoying the elite position under that ideology.)

COSTS OF "SUBSIDIZED" INFORMATION

The provision of subsidized information carries with it the necessity of meeting real, and often quite substantial, costs. "Free" information is really only free to its recipients; its producers incur extensive costs. The attainment of office in a democratically organized state in an uncertain world requires that parties incur these costs with regard to political information. Votes will be cast by consumers reflecting their acquisitions of subsidized information regarding the policies and actions of alternate parties. The resources necessary to meet the costs of these influencing activities undertaken by political parties must come from segments of the electorate which support the proposed policy positions. Parties advocating equalization could expect to see a reduction in the financing offered by wealthier agents. If parties are forced to rely extensively upon these agents for financing, and if *all* parties are similarly dependent, then no party could afford to undertake the informational campaign necessary to make equalization an issue with the vast body of voters and its implementation a pathway to office.

This potential constraint on party behavior, as was the case with those mentioned above, is reinforced in the presence of an ideology which includes a discount rate sufficiently high to raise the amount of financing of this variety which a party would require if it was attempting to utilize the issue of equalization in its pursuit of votes.

CONCLUSIONS

In an uncertain world, a lack of information as to the nature of the distribution of values and the possible gains to groups of agents from altering this distribution may result in short-run inequality, even in democratically organized political systems. Given the postulated motivations of the different groups in such a system, the long-run continuance of inequality is impossible—unless certain restrictive conditions are met. Of the four such conditions outlined, only the first, "Party Ignorance," is really devoid of ideological content. The other three conditions are all reinforced by the presence of an ideology along the lines of those discussed in the previous section. The informational explanation of inequality may be operative in the absence of an ideology but the use of informational constraints on equalization is made more efficient in terms of minimizing the costs of the affected agents by including an ideological protection of privileged positions.

CHAPTER 20
INEQUALITY
WILL ENDURE

An earthly kingdom cannot exist without inequality of persons. Some must be free, some serfs, some rulers, some subjects.

Martin Luther

If we were to rank all individuals in a given society along an index representing their control over the values of the society, values consisting of such items as "wealth," "deference," and "security," we would easily be able to distinguish between those with great endowments and those with very little. If we were then to draw an arbitrary line through this scale of rankings we could divide society into two groups, those who have, the "elite" and those who do not, the "mass." Empirical evidence would lead us to the conclusions that the mass will outnumber the elite, and then that rationality should lead this mass to take actions aimed at producing greater equality in the distribution of values in the political arena. But, in fact, we witness a continuation of inequality over the long run, despite the minor fluctuations that may occur in the structure of the distribution.

In a democratically organized state this could only take place if the larger group, the mass, were either unaware of the inequality or if it were convinced that the distribution were in some sense justified. We must conclude that the second explanation is more plausible, though it may be utilized in conjunction with aspects of the informational explanation. There exists in every human society a body of thought which unifies the population, and which coincidentally justifies the rules of operation in the society and hence the resultant distribution of values. Such an ideology is the best method, from a cost minimization point of view, of maintaining the social dominance of the elite group. The informational explanation is generally inadequate as the sole cause of the continuance of inequality; it is better suited as one of several aspects of the ideological explanation since the conditions which make it operable include the potential for further cost reductions when they are utilized in an ideological environment.

Inequalities remain over the long run—ideologies provide a low cost protection of unequal endowments from actions taken by the mass in the political realm. This fact is neither condemned nor condoned in the context of this book—it is merely noted. Ideologies may or may not be valid. Our purpose here is to show that ideologies play a real *economic* role as well as a metaphysical one. Which ideology is best must be determined by students of ethics, if such a problem can actually be objectively solved. If, as the poet claims, "Truth is beauty, beauty truth," then perhaps ideological truth, like beauty, lies in the eye of the beholder.

CHAPTER 21
SYNTHESIS
AND
CONCLUSION

The world to its discredit does not divide neatly along the lines that separate the specialists.

John Kenneth Galbraith

In the Preface to this book we outlined the path we would be taking in our exploration of some of the relatively uncharted areas of economic analysis. There were three basic questions to which we have been seeking answers. These questions and their answers are not independent, however; they are all interrelated and a real understanding of governmental actions in a market economy requires a knowledge of both the individual answers and these relationships. Let us briefly repeat the questions as we asked them in the Preface and then provide brief summaries of the answers we can provide on the basis of our analysis. It should then be possible to see more clearly the connections between the answers to the individual questions.

1. First we seek to understand the actual process by which tax and expenditure decisions are reached in the public sector. We ask not what should be; we seek only to discover what is.

   Decisions in the public realm most often center around taxation and expenditure. Some policy considerations do not directly affect taxes and purchases, but most of these will still carry economic consequences for select individuals and groups. The decisions which are reached in this sector are not the result of seeking the attainment of some universally agreed upon best state of the world. In our system they are the direct result of the often conflicting interaction of individual agents divided into four distinct groups, each with a particular goal in mind. Individuals operating in the public sector do not forego the rational pursuit of self-interest which is assumed to motivate them in the private sector. They demonstrate consistency in this regard.

   In a world of certainty, even this four-part system of decision making could lead to public decisions which actually reflect the will of a majority of the voters with regard to each issue. In a world of uncertainty where the acquisition of information is a costly process, the rational pursuit of self-interest leads to real biases being injected into this process of collective decision making.

The government, which finally makes public decisions, is subject to a high degree of uncertainty as to voters' preferences, the effects of public decisions on various groups in the system, and the costs and benefits to itself from particular issues in terms of vote maximization. Government, like all other agents, seeks to reduce this uncertainty by acquiring information at a minimum cost. To the extent that interested parties can alter the relative prices of information favorable and unfavorable to their desired end, they can influence this acquisition and with it the outcome of the decision.

Influence can also be created by trading resources for policies, either explicitly or implicitly, in order to allow government to capitalize on voters' uncertainty by influencing the expected and perceived actual utility streams derived from public action. Public decisions are effectively isolated from the abstract utility of voters. They are the result of different attempts at the production of political influence interacting with the goals of government to create a relative weighting of individuals' wants which determines, but is *not determined by,* an abstract social welfare function.

The process of producing political influence is itself a costly undertaking and can rationally be done only when the expected gains from such action exceed the expected costs. With regard to most issues it would be irrational to engage in non-voting influence. Only when an agent has a significant economic interest in the outcome of the decision, and has the ability to produce influence, will it be rational for him to enter the public decision-making process at all.

In Part I we outlined the nature of the system in which these public decisions are made. It consisted of four groups, each operating in the rational pursuit of its own self-interest, but constrained in its activities by the presence of uncertainty and the susceptibility to influence that this implies. In Part II we examined the operations of this system with regard to public purchases and in Part III with regard to the determination of tax burdens. The ability to control information prices or resources which may be used to subsidize others' acquisitions of information carries the implicit ability to affect these decisions made by government. Whenever the potential gain form such a decision is sufficiently high and the ability to influence is present, influence will be produced. Government actions will reflect the pressures placed upon public decision makers.

2. Secondly, we wish to know how this decision process affects the allocation of resources in the economy as a whole.

From Parts II and III, it is apparent that tax and expenditure decisions, both of which will carry implications for the allocation of resources, will not be based directly on consumer utility. They will depend instead on the patterns of influence placed upon the deciding group, the government. As a result, decisions in the public sector should not be expected to lead to a position of Pareto optimality that is defined by consumer preferences. Moreover, since these preferences have become at least partially endogenous, the entire concept of Pareto optimality has lost its meaning.

The allocation of resources resulting from the operations of the private market sector will reflect the initial distribution of income since it is both the desire and the ability to purchase which make demands effective. In Part IV we saw that in terms of influencing the actions of government it was also both the desire and the *ability* which made the difference, and that large economic agents had far greater ability to produce influence than smaller ones. The allocation of resources resulting from actions in the public sector will thus also reflect the initial distributions of wealth and income since our postulates of rationality and self-interest require those with the greatest ability to influence to use it to protect their positions. Similarly, the purchases made in the public sector will often reflect the desires of producers to maximize profits rather than the desires of consumers for utility. As a result, the payments made to factors of production used by the public sector will not necessarily reflect the valuations of consumers, and therefore the allocation of resources responding to these payments will not reflect these valuations either.

3. Finally, we wish to come to an understanding of the long-run implications of the answers to the first two questions. Are there any observable relationships between the operations of the public sector and the distributions of wealth, i.e., are there relationships between economic and political power?

We have just seen that the process of public decision making depends upon political influence, a product stemming from the control and effective use of scarce resources. Moreover, the allocation of economic resources among competing uses, and hence the distribution of real income among individual agents, is directly affected by the outcome of this decision making process. Under each segment of the fiscal program some individuals gain and others lose. To the extent that the ability to produce influence does depend upon the control over economic resources we would expect to see short-run political decisions tending to protect the positions of the largest economic agents when they conflict with smaller ones. Each individual decision need not reflect this tendency, but the net result of the entire tax-expenditure package should.

The extent to which public decisions can be used for the benefit of the biggest agents is limited by the degree of uncertainty on the part of the mass of consumers. Blatant disregard for their income positions and their general welfare will result in an increased awareness of the inequality in the distribution of wealth and perhaps in an increased dissatisfaction with it. Should enough voters become sufficiently dissatisfied (i.e., their gains from political action made large enough) they may use the political structure to cause a redistribution of wealth and income in their favor.

In Part V we examined the conditions which would give rise to equalization over the long run and provided an explanation of its observed absence even in democratic societies. The continuance of inequality stems from the establishment of a system of thought which justifies the existence of an unequal distribution of values. The rational behavior of individuals in a system leads to the acceptance of this ideology and to attempts to instill it in succeeding generations. Ideological justification of inequality in the distribution of values results from the rational behavior both of those who benefit most from it and of those who benefit very little. Its imposition stems from a process of cost minimization with regard to the separate self-interests of those on both ends of the scale. Without this ideology the long-run inequality we observe in societies could not long be maintained under a democratic system of political organization; with the ideology, inequality can be assured of existence and perpetuation.

The circularity of these conclusions leads to an important observation we can make with regard to the structure and operation of a market economy which contains a significant public sector. Having granted to different economic agents different "justified" positions on the scale of values, we can see that in the process we have also granted to them disproportionate ability to influence short-term tax and expenditure decisions. In their pursuit of self-interest they must use their influence to produce decisions which are favorable to the maintenance of their high position. The actions of government influence the distributions of wealth and income, and the distributions of wealth and income influence the actions of government.

In Part I we discussed the various theoretical views of government and stated at that time that a decision as to whether or not government functioned in a manner which protected property should come as a conclusion rather than an assumption. We can now reach such a conclusion. Governmental actions will reflect a tendency to protect the status quo in terms of the distributions of wealth and property in a society, no matter what the theoretical justification for those actions. This is a result of government by uncertain, self-interested men operating in an uncertain world. They are no worse than agents in the private sector, but they are no better. They function rationally on the basis of their self-interest, and *this will lead them to actions which, in effect if not in intent, protect the established distribution of wealth.*

They will be restricted in this by the necessity of providing a minimal level of satisfaction to a majority of the members of society, and in some cases this minimum may be quite substantial in absolute terms. Once it has been attained, however, actions will reflect a protection of the existing distribution of values since the patterns of influence placed upon government will exhibit a bias in this direction.

A predictable reaction on the part of the reader at this point is to claim that the analysis is being strongly critical of the society it models. Nothing could be further from the truth. The model we have developed neither condones nor condemns the situation it describes; it merely records a logical progression of thought from an initial set of assumptions to a set of outcomes. To be sure the conclusions that result are at odds with the norms established in most economic and political theories which describe how the world *should* operate, but the values which are derived from these models can only be applied externally to the analysis of our model. We have been concerned with the description rather than the design of a society. What is, is. Whether we find this desirable or not, it is imperative that we understand the forces and operations of society.

As with all pictures of human institutions and behavior our analysis rests heavily on the initial assumptions. If men are not self-interested then the model we have used is not an accurate picture of the world; but if men are not self-interested, then markets cannot function. If there is some different breed of men who alone enter politics, men who display altruism, self-sacrifice and deep-seated idealism far beyond that found in the private sector, then our conclusions need not follow. There seems to be little empirical evidence of such a difference.

The assumption of uncertainty is also essential for our system to be valid. If all men have all knowledge there is no fertile ground for influence, but experience and analysis will both show that men's choices are made in the shadowy realm of imperfect information. There is thus much room for influence and manipulation. If these assumptions hold, and if the logic is not hopelessly flawed, then the conclusions are inescapable.

With this new understanding of the political-economic structure we can now comment on some possible trends to be expected in societies such as the one in our model. For example, we can predict the effect that technological change will have. Increasingly complex technology will increasingly isolate individuals from information directly relevant to the decisions they must make. As each individual's functions and expertise become more and more specialized he will be forced to rely more heavily on external sources of information—i.e., as his personal realm of experience becomes increasingly focused, he will be increasingly susceptible to influence in matters outside this realm. If technological advance also encompasses the area of communications, the costs of subsidizing individuals in their acquisitions of information will fall, increasing the feasibility of producing influence. Technological advance carries with it an advancing potential for influence.

A second generalization we may make centers around changes in the size of economic agents. A tendency toward increasing the relative and absolute size of some agents in the economy will necessarily imply an increase in the effective weight placed on their political desires. There may of course be some circularity in this—agents large enough to effectively influence public decisions may use that ability to establish policies which in turn promote their continued growth. For the United States, with its tendency in recent years toward giant production conglomerates, the implications of this could be most important. In 1970 General Motors Corporation produced, by itself, more than the total national output of all but a handful of the world's largest countries. An economic agent of such size will wield significant political power.

The analysis we have developed need not be limited to anything as restrictive as fiscal measures. All governmental decisions are reached through the same process and are subject to the same sets of uncertainties and influences. Topics as apparently non-economic as foreign policy will nevertheless reflect the influences brought into play by those controlling resources. The recognition of foreign governments, policies regarding travel and free trade and even decisions regarding the initiation and conduct of war all arise from the operations of this political-economic interaction. It is the explicit recognition of this interaction which should stand as the central conclusion of this book.

The implicit assumption of a fixed and independent political structure underlying most economic analysis is invalid and unsubstantiated. The distributions of political power and the distributions of wealth are inexorably intertwined, even in a democratically organized state based upon a free market system. Governmental actions will preserve the economic status quo since they arise from patterns of influence generated by the operation of the economic system. In a system such as we have described, the actions of self-interested, rational agents operating in an uncertain world will—rightly or wrongly—cause the structure of political power to rise from a firm economic foundation. This structure and its foundation are inseparable.

BIBLIOGRAPHY

Adams, Walter, "The Military-Industrial Complex and the New Industrial State," *American Economic Review*, Vol. LXIII, May 1968, pp. 652–665.

Adams, Walter and Horace M. Gray, *Monopoly in America: The Government as Promoter*, Macmillan Co., New York, 1955.

Alchian, Armen, "The Meaning of Utility Measurement," *American Economic Review*, Vol. XLIII, March 1953, pp. 26–50.

Arrow, Kenneth J., "Alternative Theories of Decision Making in Risk-Taking Situations," *Econometrica*, Vol. XIX, October 1951, pp. 404–437.

Arrow, Kenneth J., *Social Choice and Individual Values*, John Wiley and Sons, New York, 1951.

Barber, Richard J., *The Politics of Research*, Public Affairs Press, Washington, D.C., 1966.

Bator, Francis, "The Anatomy of Market Failure," *Quarterly Journal of Economics*, Vol. LXXII, August 1958, pp. 351–379.

Baumol, William J., *Welfare Economics and the Theory of the State*, Longmans, Green and Co., London, 1952.

Beard, Charles A., *An Economic Interpretation of the Constitution of the United States*, Macmillan Co., New York, 1936.

Beard, Charles A., *The Economic Basis of Politics*, Alfred A. Knopf, New York, 1947.

Benoit, Emile and Kenneth E. Boulding, editors, *Disarmament and the Economy*, Harper, New York, 1963.

Bowen, Howard J., "The Interpretation of Voting in the Allocation of Economic Resources," *Quarterly Journal of Economics*, Vol LVIII, November 1943, pp. 27–48.

Buchanan, James, *The Demand and Supply of Public Goods*, Rand McNally and Co., Chicago, 1968.

Buchanan, James, *Public Finance and the Democratic Process*, University of North Carolina Press, Chapel Hill, 1967.

Buchanan, James, "The Pure Theory of Government Finance," *Journal of Political Economy*, Vol. LVII, December 1949, pp. 496–505.

Buchanan, James and Gordon Tullock, *The Calculus of Consent*, University of Michigan Press, Ann Arbor, 1962.

Buchanan, James, *Fiscal Theory and Political Economy*, University of North Carolina Press, Chapel Hill, 1960.

Cater, Douglas, *The Fourth Branch of Government*, Houghton-Mifflin, Boston, 1959.

Cater, Douglas, *Power in Washington*, Random House, New York, 1964.

Chester, Lewis, Godfrey Hodgson and Bruce Page, *An American Melodrama*, Viking Press, New York, 1969.

Connolly, William E., editor, *The Bias of Pluralism*, Atherton Press, New York, 1969.

Dahl, Robert A. and Charles E. Lindblom, *Politics, Economics and Welfare*, Harper and Bros., New York, 1953.

Dahl, Robert, *A Preface to Democratic Theory*, University of Chicago Press, Chicago, 1956.

Dahl, Robert, *Modern Political Analysis*, Prentice-Hall, Inc., Englewood Cliffs, N.J., 1963.

Downs, Anthony, *An Economic Theory of Democracy*, Harper and Row, New York, 1957.

Eisenstein, Louis, *The Ideologies of Taxation*, Ronald Press, Co., New York, 1961.

Fischer, Glenn W., *Taxes and Politics*, University of Illinois Press, Urbana, 1969.

Frey, Bruno and Larry Lau, "Towards a Mathematical Model of Government Behavior," Reprint No. 59 from Research Center for Economic Growth, Stanford University, Stanford, 1967.

Friedman, Milton, *Capitalism and Freedom*, University of Chicago Press, Chicago, 1962.

Friedman, Milton, "Choice, Chance and the Personal Distribution of Income," *Journal of Political Economy*, Vol. LXI, August 1953, pp. 277–290.

Friedman, Milton and Leonard J. Savage, "The Utility Analysis of Choices Involving Risk," *Journal of Political Economy*, Vol. LVI, August 1948, pp. 279–304.

Gillespie, W. Irwin, "Effects of Public Expenditures on the Distribution of Income," in R. Musgrave, editor, *Essays in Fiscal Federalism*, Brookings Institution, Washington, D.C., 1965, pp. 122–186.

Goode, Richard, *The Individual Income Tax*, Brookings Institution, Washington, D.C., 1964.

Goode, Richard, "Rates of Return, Income Shares and Corporate Tax Incidence," in M. Krzyzaniak, editor, *Effects of Corporation Income Tax*, Wayne State University Press, Detroit, 1966, pp. 207–246.

Gordon, Robert J., "The Incidence of the Corporation Income Tax in U.S. Manufacturing, 1925–56," *American Economic Review*, Vol. LVII, September 1967, pp. 731–758.

Greenstein, Fred, "The Benevolent Leader: Children's Images of Political Authority," *American Political Science Review*, Vol. LIV, 1960, pp. 934–943.

Hall, Challis A., Jr., "Direct Shifting of the Corporation Income Tax in Manufacturing," *American Economic Review*, May 1964, pp. 258–267.

Horowits, David, editor, *Corporations and the Cold War*, Monthly Review Press, New York, 1969.

Katona, George, "Consumer Behavior: Theory and Findings on Expectations and Aspirations," *American Economic Review*, Vol. LVIII, May 1968, pp. 19–30.

Key, V. O., Jr., *Politics, Parties and Pressure Groups*, Thomas Y. Crowell and Co., New York, 1953.

Kilpatrick, R. W., "The Short Run Forward Shifting of the Corporation Income Tax," *Yale Economic Essays*, Vol V, Fall 1965, pp. 355–420.

Krzyzaniak, Marion, editor, *Effects of Corporation Income Tax*, Wayne State University Press, Detroit, 1966.

Lane, Robert E. and David Sears, *Public Opinion*, Prentice-Hall, Englewood Cliffs, N.J., 1964.

Lasswell, Harold D., *Politics: Who Gets What, When, How,* Meridian Books, World Publishing Co., Cleveland, 1958.

Lerner, Abba P., *The Economics of Control,* Macmillan Co., New York, 1944.

Lindblom, Charles, *The Intelligence of Democracy,* Free Press, New York, 1965.

Lindblom, Charles, *The Policy Making Process,* Prentice-Hall, Englewood Cliffs, N.J., 1968.

Lippman, Walter, *The Phantom Public,* Harcourt, Brace and Co., New York, 1925.

Lipsey, R. G., and Kelvin Lancaster, "The General Theory of Second Best," *Review of Economic Studies,* Vol. XXIV, 1956–57, pp. 11–32.

Litt, Edgar, "Civic Education, Community Norms and Political Indoctrination," *American Sociological Review,* Vol. XXVIII, February 1963, p. 73.

Lundberg, Ferdinand, *The Rich and the Super Rich,* Lyle Stuart, Inc., New York, 1968.

McConnell, Grant, *Private Power and American Democracy,* Vintage Books, Random House, New York, 1966.

McKean, Roland N., *Public Spending,* McGraw-Hill, New York, 1968.

Mannheim, Karl, *Ideology and Utopia,* Harvest Book Series, Harcourt Brace and Co., New York, 1955.

Margolis, Julius, "A Comment on the Pure Theory of Public Expenditures," *Review of Economics and Statistics,* Vol. XXXVII, Nov. 1955, pp. 347–349.

Marschak, Jacob, "Economics of Inquiring, Communicating, Deciding," *American Economic Review,* Vol. LVIII, May 1968, pp. 1–18.

Marx, Karl and Friedrich Engels, *The Communist Manifesto,* Appleton–Century–Crofts, Inc., New York, 1955.

Mueller, Eva, "Public Attitudes Toward Fiscal Programs," *Quarterly Journal of Economics,* Vol. LXXVII, May 1963, pp. 210–235.

Musgrave, Richard, editor, *Essays in Fiscal Federalism,* Brookings Institution, Washington, D.C., 1965.

Musgrave, Richard, *The Theory of Public Finance,* McGraw-Hill, New York, 1959.

Niskanen, William A., "The Peculiar Economics of Bureaucracy," *American Economic Review,* Vol. LVIII, May 1968, pp. 293–305.

Olson, Mancur, Jr., *The Logic of Collective Action,* Schocken Books, New York, 1968.

Ott, David and Attiat Ott, *Federal Budget Policy,* Brookings Institution, Washington, D.C., 1965.

Pechman, Joseph, *Federal Tax Policy,* Brookings Institution, Washington, D.C., 1966.

Pechman, Joseph, "The Rich, The Poor, and the Taxes They Pay," *Public Interest,* Fall, 1969, pp. 21–43.

Peck, Merton J. and Frederic M. Scherer, *The Weapons Acquisition Process: An Economic Analysis,* Harvard Business School Division of Research, Boston, 1962.

Perry, James M., *The New Politics: The Expanding Technology of Political Manipulation,* C. N. Potter, New York, 1968.

Pickett, J. and R. L. Alpine, "Economic Knowledge and Political Behavior," *Journal of Economic Studies,* Vol. I, 1965, p. 51.

Ratner, Sidney, *Taxation and Democracy in the U. S.*, John Wiley and Sons, New York, 1942.

Robinson, Joan, *Economic Philosophy*, Doubleday, Garden City, N.Y. 1962.

Rothberg, J., "A Model of Economic and Political Decision Making," in J. Margolis, editor, *The Public Economy of Urban Communities*, Resources for the Future, Washington, D.C., 1965, pp. 1–37.

Samuelson, Paul A., "Diagrammatic Exposition of a Theory of Public Expenditure," *Review of Economics and Statistics*, Vol. XXXVII, November 1955, pp. 350–356.

Samuelson, Paul A., "The Pure Theory of Public Expenditures," *Review of Economics and Statistics*, Vol. XXXVI, November 1954, pp. 387–389.

Schettler, Clarence, *Public Opinion in American Society*, Harper and Bros., New York, 1960.

Schultze, Charles, *The Politics and Economics of Public Spending*, Brookings Institution, Washington, D.C., 1968.

Schultze, Charles, "Re-examining the Military Budget," *Public Interest*, Winter 1970, pp. 3–24.

Schultze, Charles, *Setting National Priorities: The 1971 Budget*, Brookings Institution, Washington, D.C., 1970.

Schumpeter, Joseph A., *The History of Economic Analysis*, Oxford University Press, Oxford and New York, 1954.

Scitovsky, Tibor, "On the Principle of Consumer Sovereignty," *American Economic Review*, Vol. LII, May 1962, pp. 262–268.

Sharkanskey, Ira, *The Politics of Taxing and Spending*, Bobbs–Merrill Co., New York, 1969.

Simon, Herbert J., "A Behavioral Model of Rational Choice," *Quarterly Journal of Economics*, Vol. LXIX, February 1955, pp. 99–118.

Slitor, R. E., "Corporate Tax Incidence: Economic Adjustments to Differentials under a Two-Tier Tax Structure," in Krzyzaniak, M., 1966, pp. 136–206.

Tullock, Gordon, *The Politics of Bureaucracy*, Public Affairs Press, Washington, D.C., 1965.

Tullock, Gordon, *Toward a Mathematics of Politics*, University of Michigan Press, Ann Arbor, 1967.

Weidenbaum, Murray, "Adjusting to a Defense Cutback: Government Policy Toward Business," *Quarterly Review of Economics and Business*, Vol. IV, Spring 1964, pp. 7–15.

Weidenbaum, Murray, "The Expenditure of Government Funds in the U.S.," *Public Finance*, Vol. XV, 1960, pp. 115–127.

Weidenbaum, Murray, *The Military Market in the United States*, American Marketing Association, 1963.

Wildavsky, Aaron, *The Politics of the Budgetary Process*, Little, Brown and Co., Boston, 1964.

Wood, Robert C., "When Government Works," *Public Interest*, Winter 1970, pp. 39–51.

Vickrey, William, *Microstatics*, Harcourt, Brace and World, Inc., New York, 1964.

INDEX